HOW *to* HEAR
the VOICE *of* GOD

SUSAN SHUMSKY, DD

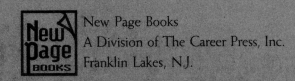

New Page Books
A Division of The Career Press, Inc.
Franklin Lakes, N.J.

HOW TO HEAR THE VOICE OF GOD
TYPESET BY KARA REYNOLDS
Cover design by Leeza Hernandez/Conker Tree
Printed in the U.S.A. by Book-mart Press

Divine Revelation is a service mark registered with the United Stated Patent Office. All of the testimonials in this book are real, but some names, occupations, or places of residence have been changed.

How to Hear the Voice of God can familiarize readers with the highly specialized, complex subjects of meditation and intuition, but in no way claims to fully teach the techniques described. Therefore, personal instruction is recommended.

How to Hear the Voice of God is not an independent guide for self-healing. Susan Shumsky is not a medical doctor, psychiatrist, or psychologist, and she does not diagnose diseases or prescribe treatments. No medical claims or cures are implied in this book and the attached CD, even if specific "benefits" or "healing" is mentioned. Readers are advised to practice the methods in this book and attached CD only under guidance and supervision of a qualified medical doctor or psychiatrist, and to use these methods at their own risk.

Susan Shumsky, Divine Revelation®, Teaching of Intuitional Metaphysics, New Page Books, and any other affiliate, agent, assign, licensee, and authorized representatives make no claim or obligation and take no legal responsibility for the effectiveness, results, or benefits of reading this book or listening to the attached CD, or of using the suggested methods; deny all liability for any injuries or damages that readers may incur; and are to be held harmless against any claim, liability, loss, or damage caused by or arising from following any suggestions made in this book or from contacting anyone listed in this book or at *www.divinerevelation.org*.

To order this title, please call toll-free 1-800-CAREER-1 (NJ and Canada: 201-848-0310) to order using VISA or MasterCard, or for further information on books from Career Press.

The Career Press, Inc., 3 Tice Road, PO Box 687,
Franklin Lakes, NJ 07417
www.careerpress.com
www.newpagebooks.com

Library of Congress Cataloging-in-Publication Data

Shumsky, Susan G.
    How to hear the voice of God / by Susan Shumsky.
        p. cm.
    Includes bibliographical references and index.
    ISBN 978-1-60163-010-0
        1. Spiritual life. 2. Listening—Religious aspects—Christianity. I. Title.

BV4501.3.S5755 2008
204'.2--dc22

                                                    2008005015

This book is an open doorway to all who seek to hear the voice of God. Welcome, all who are burdened with the cares of the world, and find the solace that you seek. You are welcome to the sanctuary of God's love. Here you will find what you have sought for lifetimes. You will dive into the heart of God and bathe in the healing pool of God's love.

"Come unto me, all ye that labour and are heavy laden,
and I will give you rest."
—Matthew 11:28

Acknowledgments

Many people have generously contributed to making this book possible. Thanks to all the staff at New Page books, especially Michael Pye, for believing in this title, and for giving me the opportunity to write about what I feel most passionately. I am grateful to Kristen Parkes for improving the manuscript and to Laurie Kelly-Pye for getting it into the hands of readers.

Thank you to the dearly beloved departed Dr. Peter Meyer, the founder of Teaching of Intuitional Metaphysics, who trained me to teach people how to open to the presence of God. Thanks to the blessed departed Rich Bell, for his magnificent healing prayers, and for teaching me how to hear the voice of God. I am grateful to Rian Leichter and P.J. Worley, for your continued support of my efforts to impart this precious teaching to as many people as possible. I thank all my human mentors, especially Maharishi Mahesh Yogi, for teaching me how to experience the presence of God. I give gratitude to the beloved effulgent beings of light, my divine spiritual mentors, for guiding me and being one with me always.

Thank you to all of my students, who make all my efforts worthwhile. I give thanks for all those who participate in my programs. And I am very grateful to those who have contributed testimonials for this book. Thank you Sean David and Melissa Morton, for your support and your assistance in getting the meditation CD produced.

Most of all, I am deeply grateful to Jeff and Deborah Herman. Thank you for your generosity of spirit, your wisdom, and your loyalty.

Contents

Preface

WHO or WHAT IS GOD?

"God has no religion."
—Mahatma Gandhi

This book is about listening to the "still small voice" of God, in whatever form you believe God to be, whether God, Goddess, Spirit, universal force, energy, or otherwise.

Let us define what is meant by the word *God*. It is an energy that permeates and gives rise to the universe. God is a non-denominational and ecumenical concept. Many people say that they dislike this word, because it evokes their early religious training, which, for some, caused pain, suffering, and guilt.

However, I believe God to be a beautiful word that embodies peace, love, joy, and wisdom. Therefore, in this book I use this word rather than *Spirit, Source, Creator, Almighty, Higher Self, Goddess,* or *Universe.* If you dislike the word *God*, then, in your mind, as you read the book, please replace it with another word of your choice.

For me, God is the all-that-is, the all-powerful, all-loving, all-embracing source of creation, which bestows love, healing, inspiration, blessings, and grace, whenever you ask. I believe in a God of love that is male and female, immanent, accessible, and alive. It holds me in loving arms and gives comfort, security, and protection.

However, if your concept of God is different from mine, this will not prevent you from successfully experiencing God and hearing the voice of God through using this book and attached CD. That is because the teachings in this book are universal.

No matter what your beliefs or background, you can hear the voice of God by approaching this book with an open mind and heart. Since 1970 I have helped thousands to experience the presence of God or to hear the voice of God, and I can help you, too.

It is important to thoroughly read and study Chapters 4 and 5 of this book before listening to the enclosed CD. Intellectual understanding is essential to building a firm foundation on which to erect the direct experience of God's presence.

Now it is time to open to the limitless possibilities of your voyage into inner space, where you will hear the voice of God, see the visions of God, and experience the loving presence of God. This is a journey of a lifetime, so be prepared to be surprised, delighted, and enlightened.

Enjoy the ride!

With love and blessings,
Dr. Susan Shumsky
June 12, 2008

~ PART I ~

DISCOVERING YOUR OWN WISDOM

Chapter 1
GOD CAN TALK *to* YOU

"Out of heaven he made thee to hear his voice,
that he might instruct thee."
—Deuteronomy 4:36

It is a rare gift to be called to hear the voice of God. By reading this book, you demonstrate faith in the prospect that two-way communication with God is feasible. This is indeed atypical. The fact that you even consider this possibility places you in a unique category of uncommon individuals. For example, were you raised in a family, religion, or educational institution where you learned that God could speak to you directly? Few people reading these words can answer *yes*.

Many people believe that God exists. Yet few believe that God hears their prayers or answers them. Fewer believe that God is accessible and can talk to them. Exceptional people are willing to allow God to speak to them directly. But only rare, extraordinary individuals act on what God guides them to do. Do you want to be one of these people? If so, you are in the right place.

We are taught from an early age that when we talk to God it is called "prayer," but when God talks to us, it is called…"schizophrenia." If you were to enter a psychiatric office today and report that God speaks to you, what would be the reaction? You would be diagnosed with mental illness and walk out with a prescription for psychotropic drugs.

We often read about murderers—even mothers who slaughter their own babies—who claim that voices in their heads told them to commit murder. We hear of cult leaders who believe that God demands that their followers commit suicide. No wonder the widespread belief is that people who claim to hear God's voice are insane.

We are conditioned to believe that the only people sanctioned to have authentic conversations with God are great prophets, saints, holy men (I emphasize the word *men*), and other holy beings who lived at least 2,000 years ago in some faraway land. These holy men wrote one book—a book literally written in stone. After that book was written, apparently, God has gone mute—and has not spoken to anyone since.

Right? Wrong.

I believe these holy men have not signed an exclusive contract with God. They have no special combination to a padlocked, hallowed safe with elite access. Some religious institutions would have you believe that they own the secret passkey and, without their sanction, no one can walk through the doorway to heaven.

Billions of people are resigned to the idea that they cannot experience God directly—certainly not while they are still breathing. Sadly, such people eagerly await death, when they will enter the glorious gates of paradise and finally catch a glimpse of God's presence. They never conceive that they could directly experience God in this body during this lifetime.

The widespread belief is that God's blessing and grace are inaccessible without a middleman, such as a pastor, minister, priest, cleric, rabbi, guru, master, shaman, psychic, channeler, counselor, or priestess. Most of these go-betweens have the best of intentions. But, regrettably, either intentionally or unwittingly, some of them become hucksters swathed in a veneer of spirituality, hawking their products to the masses.

Such salespeople have no incentive to help people hear God's voice directly. To use an analogy from the world of sales, if their customers were to have such experiences, then these retailers would soon be out of business, for their clients would "cut out the middleman" and "go direct."

However, it is my experience, and the experience of tens of thousands of people who have used the methods taught in my books or classes, that anyone can hear the voice of God directly.

THE PEARL OF GREAT PRICE

At the risk of giving away the "pearl of great price"—the most precious secret of the ages—on the third page of Chapter 1, I will tell you right now how you can hear the voice of God. This gift comes with no strings attached. You will not be required to convert to a religion, join a cult, venerate a guru, empty your bank account, or sacrifice your firstborn child. I will tell you right now how to "go direct." So here goes—a simple way to listen to the "still small voice" of God, right here and now, absolutely FREE:

Just sit down in a chair, close your eyes, take a few deep breaths, get quiet, still, centered, and balanced within yourself, and then simply—ASK. That is the entire secret. ASK. Ask a question, ask for guidance, ask for inspiration or healing. Then take another deep breath and do what I call the "Do-Nothing Program." That means, do nothing, nothing, and less than nothing. Then the "still small voice" will speak to you in your heart. You will learn this do-nothing method, called Divine Revelation, in this book.

So the key to hearing God's voice is to ASK. The trouble is that we forget to ask. Or we think we cannot ask. Or we think God is too busy for us. Is God too busy for you? Could God be too busy for anyone? If you believe God is too busy to pay attention to you, then you have a very limited idea of what God is.

God could never be too busy. God is not bound by time, space, or circumstances. Therefore, God cannot get tired or overworked. God does not only pay attention to "important" people and things. Everyone and everything is important to God. God does not play favorites. God is not available to only a select few so-called "holy" people. God is everywhere present and always available to anyone who asks.

The entire premise of this book is "Ask, and it shall be given you."[1] How to attain the requisite state of awareness, how to ask, and how to receive the message clearly are what you will learn by reading this book.

Many people have one 10-minute spiritual experience, and then spend the rest of their lives talking about it. Dozens of best-selling authors have built their entire careers upon that one time when a divine being appeared or spoke to them. However, Divine Revelation is about experiencing God whenever you want—at will. After you have learned how to hear the divine voice, you will receive spiritual experiences as often as you desire. You can call upon God and ask a question, ask for guidance, or ask to experience God, and then receive the answer or experience immediately, whenever you want—day or night. Just ASK.

Diane Wright, a dentist from Tampa, Florida, describes: *"Divine Revelation has confirmed my knowing that I can reach my Christ self whenever I want. Just being aware and knowing has increased my consciousness."*

PROBLEMS SOLVED BY THIS BOOK

Throughout 40 years of teaching meditation and intuition techniques, I have often heard the following complaints from my students, to which this book provides practical solutions:

1. "I have never meditated. Do I have to meditate in order to hear the voice of God?"

> With this book, and the accompanying CD, you can learn how to meditate and also how to hear the voice of God, whether inside or outside of meditation.

2. "Nothing happens when I try to hear the voice of God. Maybe it works for other people, but not for me. I'm just a brick wall."

> In this book you will learn ways to break down the seeming brick wall that has stopped you from hearing God's voice.

3. "How do I know whether it's really God speaking to me, or some other voice?"

> In Chapter 8 you will learn how to distinguish between God's voice and other voices in your mind, such as your ego or wishful thinking.

4. "Isn't it dangerous to listen to inner voices? What if they lead me down the wrong path? Can't I be deceived?"

> This book will help you attain spiritual discernment so you can avoid the pitfalls of psychic delusion.

5. "My negative thought-patterns, habits, and conditioning prevent me from hearing God's voice."

> In Chapter 7 of this book you will find specific healing affirmations and prayers that help you overcome negative patterns.

6. "Making the right life decisions is difficult and confusing for me."

> In this book you will learn how to ask and receive guidance from the "still small voice" of God within. That divine voice will help you make wise choices.

7. "I am offended by rules and regulations, cults, and coercive organizations."

> The universal techniques in this book impose no restrictions and are compatible with other religious philosophies, lifestyles, and personal beliefs.

8. "I don't want to work at difficult, strict, hard-to-follow disciplines."

This book is easy to understand, logical, and practical, with simple-to-learn methods requiring no previous experience, background, training, or knowledge.

SOME BENEFITS YOU CAN EXPECT

Here are a few of the many benefits you can receive by practicing the methods in this book. Included are experiences of people who have used these techniques to transform their lives.

Benefits of Hearing God's Voice

Figure 1a

1. Trusting and following inner guidance.

Linda De Narde, a property manager from San Leandro, California, says: *"I feel it is a good idea to use the voice of God as a guide. One day, I was driving in a hurry and not paying attention. I heard this sweet angel voice say, 'Linda look up,' and I did. I was heading right into a parked car on a rounded curve. I quickly swerved and could hear the minor nick as I passed the car, like a click. If I had not looked up, I would have hit the car dead center. I knew I was given grace that day."*

2. Making wise and purposeful choices with peaceful confidence.

Dan Ecklund, a physician from Foley, Alabama, says: *"Even though I find that dowsing or AK (muscle testing) can be useful confirmatory tests, I find that Divine Revelation works easiest and best for me. I have been asking questions and getting intuitive answers for 27 years, and now I can finally trust my answers! Hallelujah!"*

3. Discovering and following your true pathway, true desires, and divine purpose, in alignment with your authentic self.

Anita Foster, a massage therapist from Centerville, Ohio, says: *"The major outcome for me was a clear call to me from divine guidance that it is time to acknowledge that the reason I am here on earth this time around is to live my oneness with God."*

4. Enjoying a sense of inner happiness and peace in everyday life.

Marsha Campbell, a Unity Church administrator from Atlanta, Georgia, says: *"Divine Revelation filled me with such a feeling of peace. When I first came across it, I felt tears in my eyes. Then, as I got more into it, what came over me was immense gratitude, more tears, from so much joy of feeling 'that connection.' It was an answer to prayer!"*

5. Being more self-reliant and less dependent on others by finding answers within.

Victor Cox, from Dallas, Texas, says: *"I would like to say that since reading Dr. Shumsky's books and using her teachings, I have received many answers to questions from divine spirit regarding my life and my job. These answers have come in the form of visions, inner voices, and signs, just as she says in her books!"*

6. Achieving greater self-love, self-acceptance, and inner power.

Libby Maxey, an author from Mount Juliet, Tennessee, says: *"God-Self-Universe-every particle of everything spoke thundering through me, to me, as me, in me, around me, resonating vibrating 'I AM Thou,' and I am not separate, cannot ever be separate, from God-Self or you, or me, or the earth, or the stars, or anything again. It is so utterly simple and so extremely subtle. I can say this and mean it with my whole being: I love God, I love my neighbors, and I love my Self. I Am Thou."*

7. Attaining the true freedom that comes from direct contact with God.

Rosemarie Sanchez, from Portland, Oregon, writes: *"This realm of understanding is new for me and is exactly what I have wanted. After many years of the mainstream way of thinking, this is amazingly freeing. My word of inspiration right now is 'freedom' and even the thought of it provides the feeling of a butterfly in flight. God's love truly puts me on top of the world knowing I can create any possibility for my life I choose."*

8. Dwelling in the joyous, comforting, loving presence of God.

Michelle Engel, a schoolteacher from Ashland, Oregon, reports: *"Truly, the biggest and best miracle I've experienced is the realization of divinity within. I feel wealthy in Spirit and am completely fulfilled from within."*

9. Putting your life on track and in order.

Timothy Smith, a minister from Boynton Beach, Florida, says: *"Your teaching has made such a huge difference in my life on so many levels. It was like a lightbulb experience. All my studies of religion in my BA degree, master's, and on personal levels now made sense with the inner Christ, inner Spirit, and inner Being. Suddenly the Christ that I invited into my heart so many years ago was revealed to me. The inner Christ was there all along, I could finally see/know it as a part of me. It seems so simple yet so complex."*

10. Discovering life's meaning in spiritual enlightenment.

Albert Marsh, a retired architect from Los Angeles says: *"I experienced being 100 percent egoless. I was led into a blissful emptiness, a total silence, a total state of non-action and Oneness, and a total intense experience of the present moment. There was no emotion, no desire, no need to do anything, only a great peace. I felt like 'Albert' had gone away and I was empty of everything, impersonal. I felt as if my ego had been sent down a garbage disposal. Usually when I have a deep experience such as this, I have tears of humility, love, and joy, but there just wasn't any 'me' left to do anything, there was only pure, peaceful beingness."*

11. Knowing God and attaining God realization.

Mark Lebowitz, a physician from Dallas, Texas, says: *"I recently recalled that when I was 15 years old, my fondest wish was to know God. I just realized that I don't wish for that anymore. Because now, I think I do know Him. I am sure that I will grow to know Her more as I progress, but I have achieved my lifelong wish. Thank you, Susan."*

MY LIFE IN THE ASHRAM

I have practiced meditation and other spiritual disciplines since 1967. From 1970 to 1989, I lived in various *ashrams* (residential retreat facilities where a student studies meditation and yoga) under the guidance of Maharishi Mahesh Yogi, the guru of the Beatles and of Deepak Chopra, and I served on Maharishi's personal international staff for seven of those years.

When I lived in the ashram in India, Switzerland, and other secluded areas, I meditated from five to 20 hours per day. I sometimes cloistered myself in my room and did not appear for up to eight weeks at a time. The food was brought to my door. I often fasted for up to two months at a time. I observed silence and did not utter a sound for up to four months at a time. I observed total celibacy. I was an introvert—and that is definitely an understatement.

After spending 20 years with my eyes closed, I woke up one day and realized that I was not a spiritual person. How does a young woman meditate her brains out for 20 years and not be spiritual? Somehow, I managed to do it. You might expect a spiritual person to be kind, loving, generous, gentle, giving, caring, considerate, and patient. Yet I was not any of these things. In fact, I was a "b" with an "itch." Or an "itch" with a "b"—whichever way you want to put it.

In the ashram, every meditation afforded me the glorious experience of *satchitananda* (absolute bliss consciousness), in the state of *samadhi* (evenness of mind and stillness of body). The experience of samadhi is one of deep relaxation, profound inner peace, unbounded awareness, and transcendental consciousness.

Yet, daily experience of divine union in samadhi did not make me a kinder, gentler Susan. I was not displaying what I would call "spiritual qualities" in everyday life. Long hours of meditation did not transform my personality. What was missing was the experience of God's beloved presence and God's "still small voice."

My guru Maharishi Mahesh Yogi observed silence at the beginning of every year. He would enter his room and not appear until seven days later. Those of us on his personal staff also went into deep meditation and took silence with him. When Maharishi emerged from silence, he often mentioned something like, "I just spoke with Mother Divine, and she said...." Maharishi would then describe what the Goddess had told him.

Now, you have to understand that, as a disciple of Maharishi, I worshipped him as God. I believed he was on the highest level of consciousness and had all the answers. So, when he said that Mother Divine spoke to him, I thought, "Oh, Maharishi is so great and so high. I could never hear the Goddess speaking to me."

Like the vast majority of people, I did not believe ordinary people could ever hear God's voice. I assumed that only people like Maharishi, Moses, or Jesus could talk with God. God was certainly too busy and important to speak to common people like me. But I was wrong. My vision was very limited. Now I know better, because I have experienced the voice of God firsthand. And so can you.

I have taught thousands of people how to listen to the "still small voice" of God. If an ordinary person with no special abilities can learn to hear that voice, then you can, too. This book will show you how.

Chapter 2
HOW I LEARNED *to* HEAR *the*
VOICE *of* GOD

"I think we all have a little voice inside us that will guide us. It may be God, I don't know. But I think that if we shut out all the noise and clutter from our lives and listen to that voice, it will tell us the right thing to do."
—Christopher Reeve

The advantage I bring to my students is that I was born with no special faculties. I developed my spiritual gifts through more than 40 years of patient study, deep meditation, and spiritual practices. I traveled from point A to point B to point C. Because I walked this path myself, I know the territory and can lead others along the path.

Some gifted people claim that they had psychic gifts since birth. Because they are clueless about how their psychic abilities were acquired, how would they help other people develop theirs?

In rare cases, some people were struck by lightning and then suddenly acquired extraordinary psychic powers. How would they teach others? Would they dunk someone into a bathtub and say, "Here, stick your hand in this light socket. You can become psychic, too"?

A natural-born psychic does not describe me at all. As a child, I had no talents or inclinations in the spiritual field whatsoever. I was not born into a family of mediums and psychics. I was born into a family of skeptics and atheists. Yet, I always had a desire to communicate with God directly. That desire was eventually fulfilled. But not until I had meditated incessantly for 20 years.

Teetering on the TM Stepladder

My guru, Maharishi Mahesh Yogi, was the founder of Transcendental Meditation (TM). His teachers have taught six million people how to meditate. He controlled a colossal, worldwide organization. I lived in several of his ashrams from 1970 to 1989, including a large community in Fairfield, Iowa.

When I lived in the ashram, I loved meditation. The profound spiritual experiences that I enjoyed daily helped me develop a powerful level of awareness that has served me throughout life. That was the upside of my decades of meditation. However, there was also a downside.

As a faithful TM practitioner, teacher, and disciple, the TM creed was hammered into my brain for more than 20 years: TM is the only path to enlightenment. Maharishi is the only enlightened master. TM is your only chance for spiritual evolution. If you don't practice TM faithfully, you are doomed to lifetimes of suffering.

Like other TM teachers, I was thoroughly convinced that I was on a higher, "more evolved" level and vastly superior to the irrelevant, trifling masses of ignorant, unevolved hoi polloi, who dwelt far outside the gates of the insulated, untarnished, paradise-cocoon-safety-bubble-heavenly grace of the TM community.

The TM ashram was definitely a bubble, but it was inflated with the hot air of its arrogant, swaggering residents. I was one of them.

The TM social status hierarchy was defined by a precise stepladder, with Maharishi above the highest rung, the International Staff and other TM officials on the highest rung, TM teachers on the middle rung, and TM meditators on the bottom. When I served on Maharishi's International Staff, from 1970 to 1976, I was perched on the highest rung. However, when I left Switzerland, I slipped a few rungs down the ladder. Yet I still clung firmly to it.

One night I attended one of the frequent social events held in the homes of Fairfield, Iowa, inhabitants. There I encountered Rich Bell, a nobody whom I pegged as a bottom-feeder, crawling in the dirt below the bottom rung of the ladder.

At this party, Rich Bell resolved to convince me that he had something to teach me—a meditation technique different from TM (horror of horrors). Teach me something? Teach me anything? Ha. I know everything there is to know about meditation. The TM organization is my only avenue for learning, my only path to enlightenment, my only lifeline to God. With my nose high in the air, I flicked him away like a fly, with a flip of my wrist.

Shortly after this encounter, I was horrified to receive a phone call from a member of The Executive Board, the TM organization's governing body in Fairfield, who summoned me to his office. To describe this as a shocker is an understatement. It was more like a knockout punch. As I struggled to gasp my next breath, my heartbeat sped into overdrive and terror ripped through my bones. My mind concocted the worst possible punishment: my entry badge to "The Dome" (where TM practitioners meditated and levitated in large groups) would be confiscated, and therefore all hope of spiritual enlightenment would be dashed.

An informant apparently had reported me to The Board for organizing a New Age psychic fair at the VFW. This was an infraction of the TM organization's strict rules. TM teachers are banned from any extracurricular activity not officially sanctioned. I was accused of being a bad little girl. And The Board wanted to either slap my hands or chop them off. Which option they might choose was anybody's guess.

I do not know what possessed me to phone Rich Bell. Perhaps I was seized with a terror of drowning so immediate that I grappled for the nearest flotation device. After hearing my dilemma, Rich asked me to grab a pen and paper. Then he dictated an affirmation, which he instructed me to repeat for 15 minutes right before my meeting with The Board. Frankly, I did not know what an "affirmation" was.

I was so intimidated and frightened in anticipation of the meeting that I repeated the affirmation aloud for 30 minutes straight. Amazingly, with every repetition of the affirmation, my awareness filled with greater inner strength. By the time the meeting hour arrived, I was brimming with energy, and I was grounded and solid as the earth.

I entered the office, expecting six intimidating, glowering men ready to pounce on me. Instead I found four puppy dogs. The entire meeting turned to my advantage. Uncharacteristically polite, they ended the meeting by apologizing for any inconvenience they may have caused. I floated out of the office, high on my own energy. The entire crisis simply vanished into nothingness.

I was so impressed with the power of Rich Bell's affirmation that I asked him to teach me this new meditation practice. That is how I learned how to hear the "still small voice" of God within.

Of course, you want to know what Rich Bell's affirmation was. You will find it on page 99 of this book.

Coming Home to God

When Rich and I finally sat down together, he guided me into a meditation practice unlike anything I had ever experienced. As he led me through various levels of awareness, I saw a bright white light and later a soft azure light, otherwise known as the "blue pearl" of Lord Krishna. I expanded to levels of my higher self and visited realms of inner space that I had not previously seen on my radar map. These were celestial regions, the highways and byways of God consciousness. The "still small voice" of God spoke to me, and I received words of love, comfort, and peace.

It was fortuitous that Rich was staying in an upstairs apartment, so we had the opportunity to meditate together frequently. Then I asked him to record a guided meditation audiotape so I could practice this method on my own. He kindly made a tape, and I worked with this technique of meditation regularly.

In this form of meditation, later called Divine Revelation, it is recommended that there be a theme for each meditation. So my theme for an entire year was "deepening my inner contact." Thus I developed a powerful connection to the personal aspect of God, and I attained a level of consciousness described in ancient scriptures, which few people have ever realized. After that disciplined year of "deepening my inner contact," I began to ask questions and receive answers.

As I gradually opened to the presence, power, and glory of God, I attuned to areas of awareness never before realized. I became intimate with God in a way I could never have envisioned. This profound experience of love filled my heart with deep emotion. I returned to God, to a haven of solace where I could turn anytime for guidance, healing, comfort, and inspiration.

I was finally at home. And I was never alone again.

As my meditation practice developed, I began to teach this method. I invited Dr. Peter Victor Meyer, who was Rich Bell's teacher, to Fairfield, Iowa, and I started a meditation circle. Peter Meyer, co-author of the book *Being A Christ!*, had founded Teaching of Intuitional Metaphysics. Peter and his wife, Ann, had received this teaching from a saint believed to be immortal—

Mahavatar Babaji (pictured in Figure 2a), named the "Yogi-Christ" by Paramahansa Yoganananda in *Autobiography of a Yogi.* It was Peter who coined the phrase "Divine Revelation."

As my meditation circle grew, I soon realized that TM officials do not take kindly to TM teachers promoting meditation practices other than TM. Spies began recording license plate numbers of cars parked near my house during meditation circles. My students were called before The Board and stripped of their Dome badges. Of course, they went crawling back to the TM organization, begging for forgiveness. How could they do otherwise? They were just as brainwashed as I had been.

Before long, I was summarily banished by the TM organization and publicly humiliated and ostracized by the TM community. In 1989, due to this unrelenting censure, I was forced to sell my house and leave Fairfield.

Figure 2a

By embracing a new path, I lost everything I had believed in. I lost my position of power in the TM organization. I lost most of my friends and my home. I had assumed I would spend my entire life in Maharishi's ashram. However, there is a reason I gave up everything that I had previously held so dear. My inner guidance led me to dedicate my life to helping people contact God and fulfill their true purpose.

I now envision a world where every individual feels God's presence, listens to God's voice, and follows divine guidance. What kind of world would that be? It would be heaven on earth. Now it is my calling to assist anyone who wants to open to the voice of God.

HOW THE VOICE OF GOD LANDED A BOOK CONTRACT

On a daily basis, I do my best to listen to God's voice and follow the guidance that I receive. For example, in every step of the process of writing and publishing my first book, *Divine Revelation*, I trusted my inner voice and followed inner guidance with faith.

The book seemed to write itself, guided by the "still small voice" within. After I finished writing it, I was guided to find a literary agent. As I poured through the *Literary Marketplace* at the public library, I received a gut feeling about one agent: Jeff Herman. I knew he was the best agent for me, although it made no sense, because he represented business books, not spiritual books.

I did not have quite enough faith to send my proposal solely to Jeff. So I sent it to 30 agents. Amazingly, the first agent to answer was Jeff. He responded within two days after receiving my proposal. I signed with Jeff, and he attempted to sell my manuscript to several publishers, but he only received rejections. Then, without warning, I received a letter from the Jeff Herman Agency stating: "We are very sorry, but we have had a staff shortage in our agency, and we can no longer represent you."

I was devastated. I could not understand why God would guide me to sign with this agent, only to receive rejection. This seemed completely irrational. I decided to go into meditation to ask God what to do next.

During my meditation I received a strange message: "No, Jeff Herman is still your agent. Don't sign with another agent, and don't try to sell the book yourself." This guidance made absolutely no sense. I could have signed with one of several agents who wanted to represent me, or could have submitted my book to a small publisher. Yet I knew this strange message was true.

So I wrote to Jeff: "My intuition says that you would be the best agent to represent me." You can imagine how that went over. Many months passed, with no response. Then I finally received a letter from the Jeff Herman Agency: "We are very happy you have so much faith in us, but we still cannot represent you."

I went back into meditation. Strangely, I received the identical message: "Jeff Herman is still your agent. Don't sign with another agent, and don't try sell the book yourself." So I sent Jeff a second letter: "My intuition still says you would be the best agent for me." Months rolled by. By this time, it was too late to go back to the other agents. My manuscript sat on the table, yellowing and wasting away with cobwebs and dust.

One day, Jeff Herman telephoned me out of the blue: "We're very impressed with your perseverance. We've decided to represent you. Come to my office and meet my partner. We're going to handle your book."

I went to the office in downtown Manhattan. All the business books were stacked on the wall. I felt more than a little out of place. Jeff's partner entered the room—a beautiful woman with long, black, curly hair. I immediately felt a heartfelt affinity with her. It turned out that Deborah, who worked in the business book agency, happened to be a psychic. After our meeting, she gave me a reading. I figured that perhaps this is why I was guided to stay with this agency.

It turned out pretty well. Several months later, Jeff phoned to say that he had sold the book to Simon & Schuster. I nearly fell on the floor with shock. If you know anything about publishing, you will realize it is a total miracle that a first-time, unknown author would get a contract with the biggest publisher in the world. And even more remarkable, I know nothing about writing. I went to art college. Yet my editor said it was the very best written book she had ever edited since she started working for Simon & Schuster.

How did this miracle happen? By listening to, trusting, and following the voice of God.

"All can hear that still small voice within. Try it. Be still and know that
the I AM within you is God, the Beloved. Listen...then live by it.
It really does work."
—Eileen Caddy, co-founder, Findhorn Foundation

How God Works With You

It is easy to learn how to listen to the "still small voice" within. You learned how to do that on page 13 of this book. It is also easy to distinguish between the true voice of God and other voices in your mind, which you will learn how to do in Chapter 8. So, what is the hard part?

The challenge is to put your inner guidance into action, which is extremely difficult. For example, it was not easy to keep getting the message "Jeff Herman is still your agent," because it is out of character for me to wait patiently when I want to get something done. Yet my guidance told me to just have faith.

The reason following inner guidance is difficult is because God wants you to grow and expand beyond the limits of your ego box, to stretch the edge of your envelope. So you are given challenging assignments that help you move beyond your previous boundaries.

This process can be likened to jumping off cliffs continually, because you never know what will happen. With every leap of faith, you realize that either God will catch you...or else you have to learn how to fly really fast!

With every cliff, the leap becomes easier, and God lifts you higher each time you jump. As a result of listening to your "still small voice," trusting its guidance, and following it with faith, many miracles can take place in your life.

Travis Wyly, a chiropractor from England, Arkansas, writes: *"Thank you for the info and insights you shared about getting your book published. It was very useful to me. You inspired me to follow my heart and obey the voice of my intuition. I gave notice at my job a week ago. It was such a relief. You helped me reach a decision: To listen to and obey the voice of my inner wisdom. This life is too short to settle. I don't know what is in store for me, but I trust that the universe has something in mind, and as long as I am willing to listen and take the action, everything will fall into place. Thank you for pointing the way."*

DEVELOPING A MIRACLE CONSCIOUSNESS

Within your soul is a deep longing to return to God. Your heart's desire is to fulfill the divine plan and purpose of your life, which you are on earth to realize. Each time you listen to the voice of God and fulfill the assignment that God gives you, you raise your awareness and develop miracle consciousness.

What is miracle consciousness? It is knowing that you live in God's grace, filled with miracles and wonders every day. It is realizing that God holds you by the hand, and you are divinely protected. It is understanding that God is your only guide and you are blessed by the power of God's glory. It is dwelling under the umbrella of the Almighty, in the safe haven of God's presence. It is floating downstream in the current of God's love, washed in its beloved cleansing, healing waters. It is knowing for certain that all is in divine order.

When you have faith that you are guided by the voice of God, your life takes on new meaning and tenor. No longer are you alone in a hostile world, struggling against the tides that beat you continually against its rocky shore. Now you are swimming in the gentle, calm ocean of God's love, bathed in the holy presence of God's loving caress. You are home. You are secure. All is well.

So I invite every one of you to begin a journey with me now—a journey of greater glory than you could ever imagine. I invite you to take your first step on the road to ultimate fulfillment. You deserve to take this step. Take my hand as we now begin.

Chapter 3
The ANSWER to EVERYTHING

"Call unto me, and I will answer thee, and shew thee great
and mighty things, which thou knowest not."
—Jeremiah 33:3

Open your heart to God, and allow God to be your guide. You have all that you need within you. There is nothing to fear. The answer to everything is right here. Let your heart be an open door to the wondrous touch of God's holy presence. Let your mind open to God's radiant light, which is at the very center of your being. Let your being unite with God's divine presence, which is within you and all around you.

You are loved. You are a beloved child of God, and God is eager for you to return home. God wants you to come back to that place of perfect peace where you are safe, secure, and at rest—the holy refuge of love, harmony, and light. That place is not far away. It is right here where you are, within you. It is the dwelling place of the most high, the sanctuary of the living

God within. It is your shelter in the storm, your perfect retreat, your safe harbor.

Why would you want to return to God? Because it is the answer to everything that you have been seeking for lifetimes. Throughout your long, arduous journey, you have sought God in the arms of your beloved spouse; in the eyes of your child; in your search for wealth, power, procreation, and security. You believed these material things would bring fulfillment. Yet it was God you were seeking. You hungered for things, but the real ache in your heart was to know God. These things will never satisfy you. Only God will.

The yearnings of your heart, whether for love, money, fame, honor, glory, joy, or satisfaction—these were all cries of desperation that, at the end of the day, left you broken and in anguish. You wept tears of hopelessness in the middle of the night. Your heart was torn to shreds. Every torment of earthly life built a more impenetrable armor around your heart, which separated you from God and left you isolated and abandoned. But you are not alone. You are one with God, and God's love is within you and all around you. God loves you exactly as you are right now.

Every desire for achievement, in whatever sphere of life, is a cry for love from the depths of your soul. Yet that love cannot be found in the glories of this material world. Nor can it be found in reading books, taking motivational seminars, or practicing psychic methods. It is only attained in the ineffable love that God is. God's love is the calming ointment that mends your heart and soothes your soul. It is the healing balm that reconnects the shards of your broken spirit. It is the panacea of all ills.

> "Thou hast made us for Thyself, O Lord; and our
> heart is restless until it rests in Thee."
> —Saint Augustine

God's love is the eternal dwelling place that heals all wounds and makes all things whole. It reunites all disparities and unites them into oneness. There is no greater love than this, no greater aspiration than this, no greater fulfillment than this. God is all there is, the place of eternal content.

Wherever You Are, God Is

God's love is the indwelling Spirit at the center of your being. Wherever you are, God is. You cannot run from God, because God is right here.

You cannot turn your back on God, for God is wherever you turn. God knows all and sees all, and God is at your very core. God's love shines equally on both rich and poor, and on all races, colors, and creeds. God is present everywhere, within everything. There is nowhere that God is not. There is nothing that God is not. Because God is everywhere, and because you are somewhere, you must be exactly where God is!

"Am I a God at hand, saith the Lord, and not a God afar off? Can any hide himself in secret places that I shall not see him? saith the Lord. Do not I fill heaven and earth? saith the Lord."[1]

Because God is everywhere, and because there is nothing that God is not, then, by definition, God must be within you.

"For in him we live, and move, and have our being."[2]

Because God is within you, the answer to everything is within you. God's immeasurable love, light, power, and glory are within you. God's infinite knowledge and creativity are within you.

"The Lord is with you, while ye be with him; and if ye seek him, he will be found of you."[3]

You are the answer to everything. You are the answer to all your own questions and the fulfillment of all your prayers. Therefore, turn within and find the answers you seek. God is right here, at the center of your being, willing to give you all that you desire. Just trust in God and allow God to be your only guide. Trust that God's love, light, grace, and glory now shine upon you, answering your every need.

"Neither shall they say, Lo here! or, lo there! for, behold, the kingdom of God is within you."[4]

Allow God to lift you into the holy presence that is the answer to everything. Although you have suffered the dark night of the soul, now is the time to rejoice. For now, at the dawn, the sun of God's love shines the light of joy in the morning. God, your hope of glory, has come to take you home. Dance and delight in the presence of God, for now you are free.

Drink deeply from the pitcher of God's love, for this is the eternal wellspring that satisfies the longing of your soul. Celebrate the end of all seeking. For God's love is everything you have ever wanted, and it is more than you could ever imagine. God's love is the fulfillment of your desperate longing. It fills the hole in your soul.

"Be strong and of good courage; Be not afraid, neither be thou dismayed: for the Lord thy God is with thee whithersoever thou goest."[5]

Lift up your eyes to the heavenly realm of peace, where God dwells in glory. The divine presence is the refuge you have sought. God is your safe shelter, your Shangri-La. Rise up to welcome the streams of God's light, the waves of God's love, the glory of God's grace, the strength of God's power, and the peace of God's presence. Ascend to the mystical experience of God, where God speaks to you, just as God spoke to the prophets of old.

"The Lord spake unto Moses face to face, as a man speaketh unto his friend. Thou hast found grace in my sight, and I know thee by name."[6]

You can surrender to the living presence of God and do the will of God. You can become a mystic, a vessel of Spirit. You can be God's loving channel and do the works of God. You can fulfill your destiny as a son or daughter of the living God. As a child of God, your birthright is to dwell in the heart of God.

Now you can open to Spirit to surrender to God, see the world through the eyes of Spirit, hear the voice of God, feel the divine presence, breathe God's breath, allow your heart to beat with the heart of God, walk in God's footsteps, do the works of God, let the holy presence live through you, become all you can be, live your divine purpose and destiny, and live the mystical life of God. Now you can live the life worth living—the life divine.

Kelvin Adebuga from Nigeria writes: *"The teaching itself has had a profound impact on me. No longer do I feel that I am praying to a faraway God. The realization that 'I am one with God,' and that 'Where I am God is' changed the way I now relate to God. It is now more intimate, and [I] feel His presence more."*

You Are Worthy to Know God

At this time you might feel unworthy to receive the gifts of Spirit and the blessings of God's love, but you are infinitely deserving and abundantly worthy. As God's beloved child, you are heir to God's rich fortune of infinite blessings, and God grants you an audience whenever you ask. You are merged and one with God's holy presence. Therefore, you are not alone, and need never feel alone again.

Come home to the presence of God, where you are welcomed like the prodigal son. God greets you with open arms and takes you into its bosom. God caresses you, gives you love and peace, and showers you with blessings and magnificence.

God is at the center of your being. God is not far away, impossible to attain, or difficult to contact. You might feel blocked. Maybe you believe other people have spiritual experiences, but you never have any. However, by using the methods in this book, these seeming blockages can be removed. For you have the power to be a mouthpiece of God. You have the capacity to receive God's message, no matter what limitation you have placed on yourself, no matter what you believe is your current level of awareness.

Baldev Gambhir from Mississauga, Ontario, Canada, writes: *"I have been studying Vedanta for over 30 years. I have attended innumerable spiritual retreats over the years, but what I have learnt with Dr. Susan Shumsky is much more—way beyond what I expected. For me, all the saints appeared so unapproachable and spiritually inaccessible that I never thought I could have any personal contact with them. Through teaching me the process of 'breakthrough,' Susan made that impossibility into a divine possibility. Now I know how to get nearer to my goal of self-realization than I ever thought possible."*

Open your heart to the possibility that you can easily hear the voice of God, trust your inner guidance, and be led by Spirit in everyday life. You have the power to be all that you can be. You are blessed and beloved of God. You are bathed in the streams of God's holy light. You are filled with waves of God's love. And you are graced with God's divine healing presence. Let your heart soar into Spirit, and allow God to be your guide.

UNITING WITH GOD

Contact with God is realized through an experience called "yoga." Let us define that word. Although the discipline of *Hatha Yoga* includes physical postures, the Sanskrit word *yoga* does not mean "exercise." The word derives from *yuj*, meaning "to yolk." In other words, yoga means "unity" or "integration"— supreme union of the individual spirit (soul) with universal Spirit (God).

The state of yoga is not just for mystics of the East. It can be attained by anyone from any background or culture who wants to experience God. There is not one sole way to experience yoga. In fact, the roots of the word *yoga* and the word *religion* are identical. Both words mean "to bind" or "to yoke."

Yoga is described in an ancient scripture of India titled the *Bhagavad Gita* (*Bhagavad*: God; *gita*: song). In this dialogue, Lord Krishna (circa 3228–3102 BC), a divine *avatar* (incarnation of God), initiates his disciple Arjuna into mysteries of yoga. Krishna says: *"When the mind, thoroughly settled, is riveted in the higher self, then the person, free from yearning for all enjoyments, is said to be established in Yoga. As a lamp in a windless place does not flicker, such is like the subdued mind of the Yogi absorbed in the self. The state in which the mind finds rest, stilled by the practice of Yoga, is the state that, seeing the self by the self, finds contentment only in the self."*[7]

Here Lord Krishna describes the goal of yoga: *samadhi* (equanimity of mind and body), which is ultimate fulfillment, beyond which no greater enjoyment exists. In this state, you are fully satisfied and free from longing. Your mind is steady, like a "lamp in a windless place" or a honeybee enjoying nectar.

This settled, content level of consciousness is known as *satchitananda* (absolute bliss consciousness), which I call the "Impersonal God." It is perfection. It is absolute. It is the goal of all seeking, the end of all suffering, the ultimate realization of the truth of your being, and it is who you really are. In the ancient *Upanishads* of India, the *mahavakyas* (meaning "great pronouncements" in Sanskrit) say: "*Consciousness is Brahman.*"[8] "*I AM Brahman.*"[9] "*Thou art That.*"[10] "*All this is verily Brahman.*"[11] "*This Self is Brahman.*"[12] "That" is defined as *Brahman*—the Impersonal God.

IMPERSONAL AND PERSONAL ASPECTS OF GOD

When I lived in the ashram of Maharishi Mahesh Yogi for 20 years, I experienced the state of yoga daily and enjoyed the blissful experience of samadhi in every meditation. Yet, to my surprise, I found something lacking. What was missing from my practice was the experience of what I call the "Personal God."

The Personal God is like a loving father or mother, who brings comfort, inspiration, love, and compassion. It is intimate. It embraces you in its loving arms, holds you to its heart, and gives you solace and protection. If you ask, it will speak to you in a "still small voice." In contrast, the Impersonal God never speaks. If you think you are receiving messages from the Impersonal God, then you are deluded. For it is silent.

When I learned to contact both the Personal and Impersonal aspects of God, my experience of God reached greater depth. I realized the Impersonal God as unbounded and everlasting, and the Personal God as the comforter, the bringer of love and harbinger of joy.

Differing characteristics of the Impersonal God and the Personal God are listed in Figure 3a. Whereas the Impersonal God is infinite, beginningless, and endless, the Personal God is finite in nature. It is created and has a beginning and end (although, compared with human life, the lifespan of the Personal God is, for all intents and purposes, endless).

Although the Impersonal God is without a name, it has been labeled by many names throughout time. Some common names are listed in Figure 3b. Many of these names originate in India, China, and Japan, because in the Far East many people seek to realize spiritual enlightenment by uniting their consciousness with the Impersonal aspect of God.

Two Aspects of God

IMPERSONAL		PERSONAL
Uncreated	→	Created
Absolute	→	Relative
Unmanifest	→	Manifest
Nameless	→	Has a Name
Formless	→	Takes Form
Beginningless	→	Takes Birth
Immortal	→	Mortal
Infinite	→	Finite
Eternal	→	Lives in Time
Omnipotent	→	Has Power
Omniscient	→	Has Knowledge, Vision
Omnipresent	→	In Space and Form
Whole	→	Incomplete
One	→	Dualistic
Still	→	Active
In Equilibrium	→	In Movement
Unbounded	→	Has Boundaries
Imperishable	→	Perishable
Invincible	→	Vulnerable
Unattached	→	Engaged
Unlimited	→	Limited
Invisible	→	Visible to Subtle Senses
Imperishable	→	Perishable
Attributeless	→	Has Attributes
Emotionless	→	Loving, Merciful
Uninvolved	→	Giving, Protecting
Blissful	→	Joyful, Happy
Dispassionate	→	Compassionate
Consciousness	→	Conscious
Awareness	→	Aware
Silent and never speaks	→	Gives Messages

Figure 3a

The Impersonal God

| The Absolute |
| Brahmin |
| Satchitananda |
| Oneness |
| Wholeness |
| The Infinite |
| The Unbounded |
| The Eternal |
| Life Force |
| Unified Field |
| The Universal |
| OM |
| Tao |
| Yi |
| The Transcendent |
| Bliss Consciousness |
| Transcendental Awareness |
| Being |
| Beingness |
| Awareness |
| Cosmic Consciousness |
| Unity Consciousness |
| Samadhi |
| Satori |
| Nirvana |
| The Void |
| The Gap |

Figure 3b

The Personal God is common throughout all the world's religious traditions. Figure 3c lists many names from various parts of the world. Your personal religious tradition may or may not be mentioned on the chart.

Personal God From Religious Traditions

SPIRITUAL	God, Goddess, Lord, Creator, Almighty Anointed One, Wise One, Father God, Divine Mother Mother/Father God, Spirit, Holy Spirit, Great Spirit
CHRISTIAN	Jesus Christ, King of Kings, Lord, Lamb of God Father God, Holy Spirit, Holy Ghost, Savior, Messiah, Redeemer Mother Mary, Our Lady, Blessed Virgin, Mother of God
JEWISH	Most High, Holy of Holies, YHVH, Yaweh, Jehovah Hashem, Elohim, Adonai, Shechinah, Elohenu, Holy Spirit
HINDU	Brahma, Vishnu, Shiva, Sri Krishna, Ganesh Lakshmi, Durga, Parvati, Saraswati
EGYPTIAN	Atum, Ammon, Isis, Hathor, Sekhmut Ra, Ptah, Set, Thoth, Horus, Astarte
GREEK	Zeus, Hera, Poseidon, Demeter, Apollo, Ares, Aphordite, Hermes, Artemis, Hestia, Athene, Hephaestos
NORTH AMERICAN	Wakantonka, Wakonda, Wakan, Awonawilona, Gluskap, Nokomis Olelbis, Shakura, Tirawa-Atius, Torngasak, Sun, North Star
SOUTH AMERICAN	Pachamac, Pachamama, Maya, Auchimalgen, Viracocha, Inti Itzamna, Ix Chel, Ixtab, Wirakocha, Kukulcan, Mama Quilla
BUDDHIST	Buddha, Kwan Yin, Maitreya, Pa Hsien, Ti-Tsang Wang, Jade Emperor
JAIN	Mahavira,Vardhamana, 24 Jinas
ISLAMIC	Allah, Muhammad
CELTIC	Dagda, Danu, Angus, Brighid, Morrigan, Lug
SLAVIC	Mati Syra Zemlia, Belobog, Chernobog, Dazhbog, Mokosh
MESOPOT.	Anu, Anshar, Gilgamesh, Ishtar, Marduk, Shamash, Sin
NORSE	Thor, Freyr, Freyja, Odin, Frigg, Njord, Odin
OCEANIC	Qat, Pele, Maui, Io, Hina, Great Rainbow Snake, Wondjina
JAPANESE	Izanagi, Izanami, Amaterasu

Figure 3c

In addition to the religious names of the Personal God, there are also more generic, perhaps more secular names for this aspect of God. These names are often used in New Thought or New Age teachings. A list of what might be called "generic" names of the Personal aspect of God is found in Figure 3d.

Generic Personal God

Divine Mind
Mighty "I AM"
Higher Self
Immortal Soul
Atman
Higher Power
First Cause
Super-Mind
Over-Soul
Super-Ego
Integrator
Observer
Mind
Inner One
Superman
Inner Voice
Perfect One
Transformer
Comforter
Harmonizer
Superconscious
Intelligence
Higher Mind
Knowingness
Conscience
Inner Teacher
Inner Guru
Inner Wisdom
The Universe
The Source

Figure 3d

Your own Personal God is the God of your own understanding, in whatever form you believe God to be, whether "generic" or "religious."

Four main systems of yoga all lead to the same goal—divine union: (1) *Hatha Yoga*, the path of physical development; (2) *Bhakti Yoga*, path of devotion to God; (3) *Jnana (Gyana) Yoga*, path of discernment; and (4) *Karma Yoga*, path of selfless service. (For more information about all eight systems of yoga, read my book *Exploring Meditation*.)

The method you are learning in this book fulfills these paths by helping you experience the state of yoga. The experience of the Personal God fulfills Bhakti (devotional) Yoga, and following your inner guidance fulfills Karma (action) Yoga. The yoga asana and *pranayama* practices in my books *Exploring Meditation* and *Exploring Chakras* fulfill Hatha (life force) Yoga. Experiencing the Impersonal God fulfills the other paths.

In this book and CD you will learn how to contact both the Impersonal and Personal aspects of God. The Impersonal God brings an experience of deep relaxation, profound peace, content, harmony, oneness, bliss, perfection, and wholeness. The Personal God brings a feeling of great love, comfort, joy, happiness, security, and being at home.

THE ADVANTAGE OF DIRECT EXPERIENCE

Many people spend their entire lives studying spirituality, consuming book after book, seeking truth. They attempt to find the wisdom of the ages searching the pages of various tomes. Or, like the unruly track of a tennis ball, they chase a plethora of gurus at random, hoping to gain understanding from so-called enlightened ones.

Some people admit openly that they are seminar junkies. They boast about hundreds of gatherings they have attended with dozens of gurus. However, all the information they have acquired through books and lectures has not brought them the goal that they sincerely seek: direct spiritual awakening.

Others have taken the religious route. They attend church dutifully. They read the Bible frequently and participate in church functions. They pray regularly for themselves and others. They give generously to charity and try to exemplify the ideals of their religion. They attempt to live piously, hoping that after death they will see God in the life to come. Yet, all this religiosity has not bestowed on them the experience they so dearly desire: direct contact and communication with God in this life.

In order to fully enjoy the experience of God, it is important to gain intellectual understanding and also direct empirical experience. My guru Maharishi Mahesh Yogi used to illustrate this with an analogy:

Imagine that I showed you a strawberry. I might say, "See this strawberry. How lovely it is with its bright red color, its graceful bulbous shape that comes to a point, and the tiny yellow spots all over it. See the beautiful bright green leaves and stem. This strawberry is so luscious and succulent. It tastes a bit tart and also deliciously sweet, juicy, and sugary."

I could continue to describe the strawberry for a long time, revealing its attributes. Perhaps I could give several lectures about the virtues of the strawberry. Or I could write books describing strawberries in great detail. From my elaborate description, you might begin to understand what a strawberry is, at least intellectually.

However, until I actually hand you the strawberry, and you take a bite of the strawberry and eat it, you will never really know what a strawberry is.

Similarly, you will never know what the presence of God feels like or what the voice of God sounds like until you experience it directly. Many teachers, authors, and writers describe the presence of God, the light of God, and the glory of God. Many poets describe it much better than I ever could. However, how many of these writers can actually help you directly experience the presence of God?

"Reading about enlightenment is like scratching
an itch through your shoe."
—Roshi Philip Kapleau

"You can talk about God, and you can think about God,
but that does not bring God into your experience."
—Joel Goldsmith

The unique advantage that this book brings is not only powerful intellectual insight and discernment but also profound direct experience of God. The CD included with this book will help you have this experience.

The Difference Between Seeking and Finding

You might consider yourself a seeker, attempting to achieve enlightenment, God consciousness, contact with God, ascension, peace of mind, or another state of awareness. If so, you are not alone. Many people are seeking higher consciousness.

Some seekers are eager and filled with hope, believing that eventually they will attain the state they seek. Others are frustrated and impatient, hoping they might realize that blessed state, but doubting they could reach it. And there are the jaded. Exasperated and weary, they have given up their cherished dream in despair, believing that no one can ever achieve God realization.

I was a seeker. Earlier in my life, I sought spiritual enlightenment for decades. I believed that it was possible to raise my consciousness if I meditated regularly and strictly followed my guru's advice. Although he taught that cosmic consciousness could be achieved through his five- to eight-year plan, after spending more than 20 years under his tutelage, meditating my brains out, I eventually concluded that it might take many lifetimes to reach spiritual enlightenment.

However, through learning and teaching Divine Revelation since 1986, I have discovered an amazing secret, which I would like to share now. This is important, so pay attention:

The fact is that there is nothing to attain, nothing to achieve, and nowhere to go. The truth is that you are already enlightened right now. Your higher self is already one with God. Just lift the illusory veil that you think has separated you from God.

To understand this concept, imagine yourself climbing a ladder, the "Ladder of Spiritual Evolution." Spiritual practices, such as meditation or prayer, help you move up the ladder. As you ascend the ladder, you believe you are becoming more "spiritually evolved." You might compare yourself with other people higher or lower on the ladder; therefore, you may feel superior or inferior to them.

However, no matter how high you climb, the ladder always appears taller. As you move up the ladder, it never seems to end. There is always another rung above you. That is because this is the ladder of *seeking*, not the ladder of *finding*.

Yet there is something quite amazing about this ladder. The fact is that you have been so busy climbing, you did not notice that, no matter what rung of the ladder you have reached, you can jump off the ladder right into the heart of God at any time.

You do not need to continue climbing the ladder of seeking. At any moment you can jump off this ladder into the divine ocean of God's love, the sea of being found. The only thing separating you from this ocean is your own disbelief, your denial of God. This is called the veil of unbelief, the ego, identification, the façade barrier, psychic barrier, or the false belief in separation from God.

"Those who seek the truth by means of intellect and learning only get further and further away from it. Not until your thoughts cease all their branching here and there, not until you abandon all thoughts of seeking for something, not until your mind is motionless as wood or stone, will you be on the right road to the gate."

—Huang Po

The Divine Revelation Breakthrough Session can help you jump off the ladder and pass through the veil of unbelief, right into the heart of God.

In Part II, you will learn more about how to move through the veil that has separated you from God. You will discover how you can hear the voice of God and experience the presence of God directly.

— Part II —

Experiencing Your Breakthrough

Chapter 4

The FOUR SIGNPOSTS of SPIRIT

"I am the Christ, the Son of the Living God within me."
—Dr. Ernest Holmes, founder of Church of Religious Science

Now you are preparing to take the next step: the "Divine Revelation Breakthrough Session," which is found on the CD. Before this book was published, you could only achieve your breakthrough experience by taking a seminar or getting a session with a qualified teacher, either in person or on the phone.

However, this book has a great benefit. It is designed to help you experience the breakthrough by using the handy, special Divine Revelation Breakthrough Meditation CD, bound right into the book.

Before you listen to the CD, it is important to understand what you will experience during your breakthrough session. Therefore, please read and study the next two chapters before attempting to use the CD.

What Is a Breakthrough?

During your breakthrough session, you can break through the façade barrier, the veil of unbelief that has separated you from God, and you can directly contact and communicate with God. The façade barrier is not real. It is a false concept, an illusory wall you have placed between yourself and God. This seeming blockade is your ego or sense of individual identity, also called "identification."

If I were to ask the question, "Who are you?" perhaps you would answer, "My name is so-and-so. I live in such-and-such town at this address. I have this job. I am married to this person and have these children. I have this education and these hobbies. I follow this religion. That is who I am."

But is that who you are? Are you your occupation, family, or religion? You may have identified yourself as your history and activities. However, you are not these things. Perhaps that is who you *think* you are. But that is not who you really are.

You might see yourself as a powerless victim of circumstances, possessing scanty resources, knowledge, opportunities, and possibilities. Perhaps who-you-think-you-are is a limited being, crippled by situations and conditions. But that is not the truth.

Who-you-really-are is a divine, all-knowing, all-loving, all-powerful spiritual being—immortal, unlimited, and multidimensional. You are much more magnificent than you could ever imagine. In fact, you are created in the image and likeness of God, filled with glory, blessings, and wonders.

"Turn thy sight unto thyself, that thou mayest find Me standing within thee, mighty, powerful, and self-subsisting."
—Bahá'u'lláh

Through free will, you are already creating and changing conditions in your life and the life of others. Therefore, you have the power to transform and heal yourself, your community, your country, even the planet. In fact, you can do anything, through the power of your intention, in cooperation with God.

You may have identified yourself with narrow boundaries, but you are not bound. Your breakthrough session can help you overcome your limited perspective and realize the truth. By breaking through this false veil of limitation, you can realize who you really are—a being of pure divine energy, one with God, vibrating and radiating God's love, filled with God's grace, and bathed in God's glory.

WHAT HAPPENS DURING YOUR BREAKTHROUGH

Your Divine Revelation Breakthrough Session will help you experience God directly. There are four goals of the session: (1) Presence of God, (2) Name of God, (3) Signal of God, and (4) Message of God. As a result of your breakthrough, you will begin to recognize God's presence through these four signposts. The remainder of this chapter explains these four goals in detail.

Four Signposts of Spirit

1	**PRESENCE OF GOD**	**Inner Contact**
2	**NAME OF GOD**	**Inner Name**
3	**SIGNAL OF GOD**	**Inner Signal**
4	**MESSAGE OF GOD**	**Inner Message**

Figure 4a

1. Presence of God

The first goal of your breakthrough session is called the "Presence of God," or "Inner Contact." This is direct experience of God's loving presence—a feeling of being at home in the heart of God. When I first learned Divine Revelation meditation, I found great comfort and solace, because I would never be alone again. When you are in contact with God, you will receive ecstatic feelings and blessings, such as:

- Unconditional Love
- Peace, Tranquility, Serenity
- Comfort, Protection, Security
- Confidence, Assuredness
- Joy, Happiness, Ecstasy
- Streams of Divine Light

- Waves of Divine Love
- Inner Strength, Power, Energy
- Contentment, Fulfillment
- Grace, Blessings, Glory
- Oneness, Wholeness

The most important of these feelings is oneness and wholeness. Such a feeling helps you to identify that you are truly sitting in the lap of God's love.

Divine Revelation Experiences

The following are comments from students who describe their break-through session. These testimonies offer tangible evidence of the divine presence as a palpable experience.

Juan Martinez, program evaluator from Saint Paul, writes that he sensed *"a feeling of joy coming in waves, the realization that God is here and now, not there and later."*

"I realized that God is in me and I am in God, and so I am loved completely and unconditionally, and loving in the same way," recounts Nevada City, California, mortgage broker Rob Bell.

Paul Campbell, a civil engineer from Singapore, describes: *"The Holy Spirit came to me and infused me with the love and power of God expressed as a radiant white light and a feeling of true bliss. I received love, peace, and encouragement from the Holy Spirit—oneness with God and the universe."*

John Baxter, an accountant from Seattle, reports: *"As I went deeper, I began to get a sense of wonderment about how God feels. After coming out, I felt a very solid physical stillness, like no action on my part was needed other than to be."*

As you meditate with the Divine Revelation Breakthrough CD, you can experience peace, relaxation, and perhaps other feelings associated with the holy presence of God. However, it is vital to have no particular expectations as you listen to the CD. Your experiences might be exactly the same as you usually have during ordinary meditations.

2. Name of God

The second goal of your breakthrough session is called the "Name of God," or "Inner Name." Everything in creation has a name or vibrational energy (sound), and a form, or energetic signature (sight). String theory in quantum physics tells us that the universe consists of subtle vibrations that are undetectable even with the strongest microscopes.

It is said in the West: *"In the beginning was the Word, and the Word was with God, and the Word was God."*[1] *"By the word of the Lord were the heavens made; and all the host of them by the breath of his mouth."*[2]

In the East it is stated: *"As an immortal principle, I am formless, and as Creator, I possess a form. As an eternal principle, I have no beginning, middle or end; my name is OM."*[3] *"The syllable OM is what is called the word. And its end is the silent, the soundless, fearless, sorrowless, joyful, satisfied, firm, unwavering, immortal, immovable, certain (Brahman), called Vishnu."*[4]

The vibration OM is believed to be the fundamental sound from which all 50 letters of the Sanskrit alphabet arise. These seed sounds originate all sounds, and thereby generate the entire universe. The ancient scriptures of India say that OM is "the first," the primordial vibration underlying all other vibrations and therefore all forms.

As you learned in Chapter 3, the Impersonal God is without name, form, or attributes. But the Personal God is known by many names. See Figure 3c on page 35 for a list of names of God from various cultures. Some of the most common are as follows:

- God
- Lord
- Holy Spirit
- Jesus Christ
- Mother Mary
- Allah
- Lord Krishna
- Lord Buddha
- Hashem

When you meditate using the enclosed Divine Revelation Breakthrough CD, you will contact one particular aspect of God—namely, "Holy Spirit" in female form. I have painted a picture of her as seen in my inner vision in Figure 4b. However, you might envision her entirely differently.

The Holy Spirit is traditionally depicted as a dove shining rays onto the earth. In this painting, a female figure represents the feminine aspect of God. The female Holy Spirit is also known as AAA, the letter "A," first letter of the alphabet, representing oneness, three times—the Holy Trinity. She stands on the sun of the omnipresent eternal Godhead. She is depicted in white, symbolizing absolute purity, radiating unconditional love.

IMPORTANT: It is essential to understand now, at the outset of your study, that you do not need more than one inner name to successfully hear the voice of God. For instance, if you only feel comfortable with the name God, or the name Universal

Figure 4b

Mind, or Jesus, or Buddha, or Holy Spirit, you can ask to communicate solely with that one being to receive all your divine messages. You do not need to contact any other aspects of God.

Divine Revelation Experiences

Lenda DeAnn, a baker from Grass Valley, California, describes her breakthrough: *"I met a man in a burgundy toga with gold around his head. He said he was my guardian angel and his name was Archangel Michael."*

Melanie Gonzalez from West Covina, California, writes: *"I saw an eye in the middle of our meditation circle, floating in the air looking down on all of us. Susan said I was receiving a signal. Then she instructed me to ask the divine being who it was and to get the name. I saw three words typed out below the eye: 'I AM God.'"*

3. Signal of God

The third goal of your breakthrough session is the "Signal of God," or "Inner Signal." A signal is a sign that you are in contact with a particular aspect of God. Every divine being that you communicate with will give you a specific name and a corresponding signal so you can identify it.

Undoubtedly, you have already experienced a signal sometime in your life. It was an experience that uplifted and touched your soul. Here are some possible examples:

- **Music:** You heard uplifting music on the radio or at a concert that really moved you and perhaps brought you to tears.
- **Nature:** While walking through the woods, you suddenly sensed an upsurge of energy or felt at one with nature.
- **Art:** You were at an art museum and a particular painting kindled your spirit or opened your eyes to new possibilities.
- **Religion:** At your house of worship, the stirring words of the Sunday message touched your soul and attuned you to the harmony of the universe.

- **Universe**: A beautiful sunrise over a vast ocean or a dramatic meteor shower reminded you of the unlimited cosmos.
- **Service**: You were helping a friend in need, or doing volunteer work that inspired you and made you feel closer to God.
- **Speaking Truth**: You spoke some profound words of truth, and wondered, "Where did that come from?"
- **Athletics**: You pushed the edge of your envelope in an athletic performance, and, as you broke your personal record, you felt elated.
- **Literature**: A book that you read inspired and uplifted your spirit, and you were transformed.
- **Drama**: A dramatic performance or movie really moved you. Your emotions were aroused, and your heart was touched.

At the very peak point of such experiences, at your most thrilling "aha" moment, a special feeling went through your body or senses. Your hair stood on end; you got goose bumps, rushes of energy, or surges of heat. You felt electrified, animated, illumined, and uplifted. Perhaps you realized, "Now I know the truth." You felt touched by God.

Have you ever experienced such a sensation? If so, that is one of your signals—a sign indicating that a specific aspect of God is present.

Such exquisite incidents of heightened spiritual awareness may be familiar to you. At such times, you might even remark, "Oh, I just got chills going up my spine," "I'm getting truth chills," "That gave me goose bumps," "My hair is standing on end," "Now I can see it all so clearly," "Now I see the light," "I feel good vibrations," "I'm on top of the world," "That gave me a warm glow," "My heart is touched," "That moved me," "I am thrilled," "That rings true," "That feels solid," "It just feels right," or "I'm in sync and in harmony."

These peak sensory experiences are called "divine signals." They are truth signs—indications that you are in tune with Spirit. A signal is like God knocking on your door, saying, "Wake up and pay attention. I am giving you this signal so you know I am present."

Each inner name that you contact has a specific corresponding divine signal. For example, Holy Spirit is one name you might contact, commune with, or converse with. Holy Spirit will give you a unique, recognizable signal. However, Holy Spirit will give you a different signal from another aspect of God, such as Jesus or Lord Krishna. Your signal for Holy Spirit, however, is unique and different from another person's Holy Spirit signal. The divine signal indicates which aspect of God is present and ready to give you a message or experience.

Familiar Signals

Your signals may be so familiar that you do not even notice them. They are simply part of your everyday existence. Some students expect a flashy, holographic, multidimensional experience during their breakthrough session. So, when they get the same old experience that they receive every time they meditate, they are surprised.

Georgia Rhinebeck, a writer from Cleveland, describes: *"I identified the signal I've been receiving for years to be the Holy Spirit, and I believe I knew that in the back of my mind."*

"I have for a long time been aware of a tingling sensation over the crown of my head being a sign of connection, yet I am now aware of the distinctions of sensation and positions of signals for different divine beings," says Susan Morton, a therapist from Phoenix.

Charles Wright, a physician from Tampa, writes: *"I had been getting signals but never recognized them before. I didn't know what they were."*

Many people think everyone experiences life the same way they do. Therefore, you might imagine the word *meditation*, or *signal*, means the same to you as it does to others. Also you may think everyone's experience of meditation is like yours. This is not true.

To illustrate this point, I was attempting to verify the divine signal for a woman from Staten Island, New York. I asked her what she was experiencing. She replied, "Inner peace." I instructed her to take a deep breath and go deeper. Again I asked her to relate her experience. She reported, "Peace." A third time I told her to take a deep breath. Again she said, "Peace." Then I asked, "Where is this feeling of 'peace' located?" She promptly answered, "It's that feeling of the cloak around my shoulders, just like everybody gets when they meditate." I explained that everyone's experience of meditation is unique, and her signal was the peaceful, protective sense of a cloak around her shoulders.

Some students insist that nothing is happening during their breakthrough session. However, when I probe more deeply, I discover they are taking their signal for granted, because they have received it for decades, yet never recognized it as a signal. If your signal is very subtle or overly familiar, then you might dismiss its significance.

Ways to Get Signals

You have many inner divine signals that you can now begin to identify. Divine signals come in one of six ways, through your subtle senses, by (1) sight, (2) sound, (3) smell, (4) taste, (5) feeling, or (6) body movements. The following is an explanation of various kinds of signals:

Six Ways to Get a Signal

1	SEEING	Visual
2	HEARING	Auditory
3	SMELLING	Olfactory
4	TASTING	Gustatory
5	FEELING	Kinesthetic
6	MOVEMENT	Kinetic

Figure 4c

1. Seeing a Signal

When you "see" a visual signal, it likely appears in your inner vision with your eyes closed ("inner clairvoyance"). Few people see signals with their eyes open ("outer clairvoyance"). Here are some examples of visual signals:

You might clairvoyantly see a pleasant vision in your inner eye. It may be a light of a particular color in a specific place, seen in your inner vision, body, or an energy center. The light might be white, gold, blue, violet, or another beautiful color.

Or your signal might be a beautiful symbol, such as a rose, tree, flower, geometric shape, Star of David, cross, sunrise, mountain, sacred place, or another pleasant vision. You might see a face or figure of a deity, a saint, or a beautiful, shimmering angel. Perhaps you see Jesus, Buddha, Krishna, or another divine being.

Divine Revelation Experiences

"My signal for Holy Spirit was a white dove outlined in blue above my head, sending a ray of golden light through my body," writes Marianne Remington, an editor from New York City.

John Tang, a physician from San Francisco, reports: *"When calling upon Kuan Yin, I saw a patch of dark, clear, blue sky growing brighter, followed by white clouds floating in the sky. When I asked Kuan Yin to confirm it was the signal, the clouds grew more. It was a very pleasant feeling."*

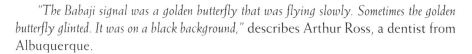
"The Babaji signal was a golden butterfly that was flying slowly. Sometimes the golden butterfly glinted. It was on a black background," describes Arthur Ross, a dentist from Albuquerque.

2. Hearing a Signal

An auditory divine signal is "heard" in your inner ear ("inner clairaudience"). It would be rare to hear signals audibly ("outer clairaudience"), but it happens on occasion.

You might hear a pleasant sound in your mind. Perhaps you hear a tone, bells, chimes, harps, celestial flutes, violins, celestial symphonies, music of the spheres, angelic choirs, chanting, falling rain, rustling leaves, rushing water, wind, ocean waves, the sound of the universe, a hum or "OM," or another sound.

Divine Revelation Experiences

Virginia Goodwin, an artist from Denver, narrates: *"When I got my signal, I heard an exquisite humming sound that can only be described as celestial."*

"My signal for Lord Krishna was the heavenly sound of a flute," describes Arthur Schwartz, a teacher from Billings, Montana.

A writer from Fort Wayne, Indiana, named Charles O'Hara reports: *"My signal was a lyre played by an angel. I could hear its music, which was thrilling."*

3. Smelling a Signal

Olfactory signals are celestial fragrances that you "smell" with your inner senses. This is called "clairgustance." As you detect these sweet scents, you might look for someone wearing perfume near you, but no one is. Instead, your inner sensing is picking up a heavenly aroma.

You might sense a lovely fragrance, such as rose, jasmine, lilac, gardenia, lavender, honeysuckle, pine, eucalyptus, sandalwood, orange, lemon, vanilla, peach, cinnamon, nutmeg, or some other charming scent. It might be a recognizable or unrecognizable pleasant aroma.

Divine Revelation Experiences

Mark Hebert, massage therapist from Fort Lauderdale, Florida, recounts: *"I opened and received an olfactory sensation. This was a new experience for me, a clear distinct smell of rose essential oil."*

"I experienced my body moving back and forth along with the strong scent of flowers," relates Emelia Lau, administrative officer from Toronto.

Harsharan Kaur, a student from New York City, describes: *"When Holy Spirit came, I smelled a beautiful, sweet-smelling fragrance."*

4. *Tasting a Signal*

Gustatory signals are subtle tastes detected somewhere in your mouth or throat. It tastes as if you have eaten something sweet, although you have eaten nothing. This is called "clairgustance."

You might taste a sweet, pleasant flavor. It may taste like something familiar, such as coconut, banana, carrot, apricot, orange, peach, pear, raspberry, pineapple, tangerine, grape, cashew, almond, rosewater, milk, or another pleasant, ambrosial taste. Or it may be a completely unfamiliar and unrecognizable yet luscious flavor.

Divine Revelation Experiences

Joshua Montross, construction worker from Asheville, North Carolina, describes: *"I noticed my higher self came as the taste of strawberries on my tongue."*

"My signal for Lord Shiva was clear—I never tasted anything like that, something creamy and delicious," writes receptionist from Iowa City, Vanessa Klepper.

Dawn Pelissini, a schoolteacher from Dallas, Texas, recounts: *"When I went into the meditation, it was like my mouth suddenly filled with something sweet. I couldn't recognize it, but it gave me joy."*

5. *Feeling a Signal*

A kinesthetic signal is a subtle feeling in your body. This is called "clairsentience." You might receive an unusual pleasant sensation in a particular part of your body or all over your body.

Perhaps you sense energy moving in your body. You might feel heat, warmth, or a cool breeze. Extremities, such as your arms, legs, or toes, might tingle or pulsate. Maybe a rush of energy or tickling sensation travels up your spine. Energy or electricity might course through your body. You may feel something surrounding, cloaking, or protecting you. Or you might sense something literally touch your body. Perhaps your body seems to change size or shape. It may appear to expand or contract, become numb or disappear. You might lose body sensation altogether. The body boundaries could dissolve. You might experience tears of joy. You may get strange sensations, such as spiraling or another geometric shape. Or your signal might be another bizarre experience that is difficult to describe.

Divine Revelation Experiences

Annamaria Spielman, a textile stylist from Massapequa, New York, experienced her signal as *"vibrations and heat upon crown of my head, pulling of hair, and feeling as if someone lifting my head from my spine."*

"I felt a tingling sensation starting from my legs and swelling into my upper body. At times this energy was intense. I was weeping and shaking," writes Alex Huntington, an engineer from Oviedo, Florida.

Marshall Sass, commodities trader from Austin, Texas, describes: *"The divine Spirit signal was a warm, expansive feeling in my heart and lower chest. The warm feeling inside me was incredible. The divine Spirit told me how to deal with life's problems by staying grounded in the glow of divine Spirit. I was told how to deal with uncertainty: 'Pray for courage, and let the warm glow of divine Spirit carry you through.' A big thing I learned was that I can feel God inside of me, as a real, powerful presence, not as some abstract, faraway thing."*

6. Body Movement Signals

When you get a physical movement signal, a body part or your whole body moves, rocks, or shakes. This is nothing to fear. It is a sign that God is present.

Perhaps your head rocks or swivels back and forth. Your head or whole body might make circular movements. Your head may move or tilt in a particular direction, or bob or rock. Your entire torso might rock or move. Your eyelashes might flutter. Perhaps your head tilts backward or tips to one side. Maybe your eyes roll back in their sockets. An extremity might lift, rock, or move. Perhaps you appear to dance. You may smile or assume another facial expression. Particular muscles might move or twitch. Your whole body might rock, shake, or quake. Remember the Shakers and Quakers? There is a reason they were given those names.

Divine Revelation Experiences

Iris Hatch, housewife from Philadelphia, recounts: *"I felt my eyelids fluttering and also felt chills or goose bumps running up and down my entire body when I called upon Jesus."*

"My signal from Holy Spirit was head tipping to the right and chills in my calves," reports Carolyn Anderson, an administrative assistant from Seattle.

Sherry Rawlings, a schoolteacher from Houston says: *"My Holy Spirit signal was energy moving up my spine towards my head and my head tilting backwards."*

Meanings of Signals

Sometimes your signals have significant meanings that touch your soul personally and eloquently. They can be constant, loving reminders of a particular teaching that God is imparting to you. Here are some experiences of my students:

A famous reflexologist from Chicago writes: *"Hashem came with a yellow orange light and said, 'Let in my love, light, joy, and peace, and let go of fear.' When Babaji gave me a signal of a warm smile, he told me that the smile will win worlds for me and heal many. With Konar, I could feel breath out of my lips and vibrations around my mouth. The message was that I will express myself through speaking to many."*

Retired teacher from Tucson, Rose Marcus, reports: *"I got the signal—a warm feeling in both my hands. It gives me the impression that God is telling me I have healing hands. I can help many people."*

Speaker and stress management consultant from Chicago, Geraldine Cunningham writes: *"The Holy Spirit represented first with a pole of turquoise blue light, followed by a ball of gold light, which got brighter and with which I became surrounded and immersed. The pole of blue light resonated. When I asked what the pole symbolized, the message came, 'I am the life force.' When I asked what the ball of gold light symbolized, it came through as 'energy vibrating in form.'"*

Inner Signals I Have Been Receiving

1. SEEING	
2. HEARING	
3. SMELLING	
4. TASTING	
5. FEELING	
6. MOVEMENT	

Figure 4d

Recognizing Your Signals

Your divine signals are consistent and never change. Perhaps you are already getting particular signals in meditation repeatedly. What signals are you receiving? Please use the chart in Figure 4d to list the signals that you have been seeing, hearing, smelling, tasting, or feeling, or your body movements. Later, as you experience your Divine Revelation Breakthrough Session, you will begin to discover specific inner divine names that correspond with these signals.

4. Message of God

The fourth goal of your breakthrough session is the "inner message," or "Message of God." This message is received in one of three ways: seeing, hearing, or feeling. Some people are naturally more visual. Others are auditory. Still others are kinesthetic. You will receive your divine messages through the subtle sense that is most natural for you.

1. Seeing the Message

Visual, Clairvoyant: Your message might appear as a motion picture or drama in your inner eye. Maybe you will see a personal, meaningful vision. For example, if you ask the question, "Is it wise to accept a particular position with a company?" your answer may be a vision of a large, imposing double door opening wide with a bright light streaming through the doorway. You might interpret that as an affirmation for you to seize this positive opportunity. You will receive this vision from a specific aspect of God within you.

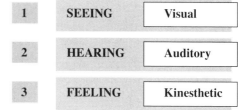

Figure 4e

Divine Revelation Experiences

Melanie Gonzales of West Covina, California, describes: *"Immediately going into the guided meditation with Susan, I saw a crystal ball. Below it was a big book opened from the middle. I didn't understand the meaning. I kept asking my question, 'What is the next step for me to take for my highest good?' and the same images remained. At one point, the image got bigger, right in front of my face, close enough for me to think, 'How much clearer do you want this message to get?' After the meditation, as each member shared their message, I suddenly realized that my images resembled the book I brought with me on the retreat—The Crystal Bible. I felt a surge of jumping joy because 'I just got it!' I thought that was way cool."*

Stuart Van Niekerk of Scotland writes: *"I had a vision of Jesus. He was taking communion, holding his finger up to his mouth, saying 'shhhh.' I realize that he is saying: 'You are healed. Just accept it. No need for chatter, talks, and so forth. Believe it and leave it.'"*[5]

Steve Ziebell, medical researcher from Iowa City, writes that he saw a *"vision of a human on fire with a golden light. It seemed like I went through a clearing and the message was this light is the being of each moment and is always there. I feel a foundation has been created for Christ love to flow through me into the world."*

2. Hearing the Message

Auditory, Clairaudient: The message might be heard as words in your mind. To understand this, imagine that you have the thought, "I have to go to the grocery store." When you think such a thought, you are hearing words in your mind with your inner ear. That is an auditory experience. Similarly, if you hear God say to you, in your mind, "I love you," that is a clairaudient impression—an auditory message, which comes to you just as other words come into your mind.

Divine Revelation Experiences

A registered nurse, Charles Mossey from Milwaukee, writes: *"The message I received was, 'Charles, you are truly blessed. Your body is being healed. Trust and have faith in me.' I asked the question a second time and got the same response."*

Ted Lisky of Portland, a real estate developer, describes: *"I ended my meditation saying 'I love you' and I distinctly got the message back 'God loves you.' Then my eyes filled with tears and I felt love and release. When I opened my eyes, tears rolled down and afterwards I cried. It was very moving."*

Cattel, an astrologer from Las Vegas, describes: *"Babaji said, 'I am the light incarnate. Divine sparks of light igniting other sparks of light—all in this room are light and when they leave, they ignite others.'"*

3. Feeling the Message

Kinesthetic, Clairsentient: You might get a gut feeling or feel led in a certain direction. For instance, if you get a strong impression that someone is good for you, then you might be prompted to become more intimate with that person. This is sometimes called "following your heart," "following your bliss," or "going with the flow." Another example may be a deep sense, or a positive experience, feeling, or emotion. For instance, if you ask a question about a lawsuit, and then you receive a deep, abiding feeling of peace, you might interpret the answer to mean that all is well and you can be at peace about the situation.

Divine Revelation Experiences

Elizabeth Laczynski, a fitness consultant from Des Moines, describes *"a feeling of total peace, comfort, and security that will always be accessible to me and all others who choose to see it. The presence of great love and joy that made me just want to smile from inside to out and continue in its existence."*

"A feeling of ecstasy infused me, and I felt totally overwhelmingly loved. I was lifted and taken care of and belonged—a part of the Holy Spirit. I felt cleansed and healed as a child of the Holy Spirit. I felt the overwhelming wisdom and power of the Holy Spirit, a bright golden light. I felt tremendous love. I also felt the Christ Spirit, a pure tender love. And the total stillness of mind brought a relaxation and complete peace that is ineffable bliss and serenity," Cheryl Fenster, a legal secretary from Santa Barbara, reports.

Katie Formento, a teacher from Las Vegas, writes: *"I felt a stimulating warm spiritual feeling penetrating my entire body. I felt God's light of protection all around me. A sense of peace, balance, and harmony. A feeling of assurance that God dwells within us and that he will always be here to guide, protect, and inspire me."*

IMPORTANT: The Message Is NOT the Signal

Please do not confuse the message with the signal. A signal is nothing other than a badge to identify a particular aspect of God. For example, if your divine signal for Holy Spirit is a white light in your forehead, then that signal will appear every time Holy Spirit is present. A signal is consistent, reliable, and never changes.

In contrast, a message is not an identifier. It always changes, and it always has a particular meaning. It is an answer to a question or another meaningful communication from God.

For instance, if you ask a question about a particular relationship that you are considering pursuing, and you receive a vision of a large, pink glowing heart, then that vision is not a signal. It is a message, because it has meaning, and it answers your question. You will likely never get that vision of the pink heart again. It is fed to you only for the specific purpose of answering that one question.

God can speak to you in myriad ways. Some of these are experienced internally, in deep meditation or in your mind. Others are signposts that appear in your outer environment. This book focuses on your internal experience of the presence and message of God. To learn about more ways to experience the message of God, please read my book *Divine Revelation*. Some of these ways are listed in Figure 4f on page 59.

Divine Revelation Experiences

Here are a few comments from students who describe their initial experience of their Divine Revelation Breakthrough Session:

Maggie Hux from Canada says: *"This has been a huge shift in my spiritual development—the biggest single change in my spiritual life over this past decade. When I did the session with Susan, she did not know me at all. We did no talking beforehand. It was awesome to make contact with my inner guidance. But even more was how specific and detailed the guidance came through Susan. Being a naturally doubtful person, it was perfect. Since that time, I have gradually learned to receive clear guidance through meditation, and it has revolutionized my life."*

An administrative officer from Sacramento, Bonnie Talbot writes: *"I feel a sense of peace, quietness in my mind, that I do not experience in any other meditations. My mind did not wander."*

Manuel Zambrano, a bus driver from Victorville, California, describes: *"I am filled with energy. I had a wonderful experience. I learned to identify within my body the presence of Jesus. I got it in front of my forehead. It's a kind of purple light that flowed or flux like*

Ways God Speaks to You

1	**Seeing Divine Visions**	**Visual**
2	**Hearing God's Voice**	**Auditory**
3	**Feeling God's Promptings**	**Kinesthetic**
4	**Divine Dreams / Deja Vu**	**Multi-sensory**
5	**Signs and Omens**	**Multi-sensory**
6	**Divine Visitations**	**Multi-sensory**
7	**Intuitive Kinesiology**	**Kinesthetic**
8	**Prophecy**	**Multi-sensory**

Figure 4f

an 'ojo de agua.' An 'ojo de agua' in my country is like a soft stream, or oozing of pure clear water that gushes from underneath the ground. Imagine that, but in the form of light. The message was very short and simple too. I heard these words: 'Know that I am Jesus, and I love you, and I am here whenever you need me.'"

"My spirit is joyful and uplifted. I'm feeling gratitude that I have a connection with God," describes Suzan Habib, archeologist from Sag Harbor, New York.

Thaddeus Timothy Sun, a student from Singapore, reports: "The experience of communing with God was profound. The Holy Spirit came down upon me like currents of electricity. With it came a wonderful feeling of intense love, power, and joy. I could feel God's powerful presence enveloping me. All the questions I asked were answered through my higher self. I was overwhelmed with peace and love."

Joyce O'Malley, telecommunications technician from Chicago, describes "feeling of great calm and oneness of being. I feel energized and alive, more than I have for years."

"I felt weightless and my skin didn't exist anymore, as if the energy inside me was flowing with the universe," Roy Efferin, a businessperson from Australia, writes.

Seattle retailer Barbara Canning writes, *"It was as though I was that being of light permeating throughout the self and I was the vehicle through which the energy flowed, and felt as though the light of the sun was dancing with delight."*

ASK, AND IT SHALL BE GIVEN YOU

Remember that the entire premise of Divine Revelation is one thing: "Ask, and it shall be given you."[6] Therefore, whenever you get a signal, ask for the name. When you get a name, ask for the signal. When you get a signal and a name, ask for the message. When you get a message, ask for the name and the signal.

Find out who is giving you this message. Discover who is giving you the signal. Identify who or what you are contacting. The names and signals help you recognize which specific aspect of God is present. That is why they are important.

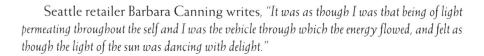

In the next chapter, you will learn more about the Divine Revelation Breakthrough Session and what will happen when you use the CD included with this book.

Chapter 5
The DO-NOTHING WAY
to MEDITATE

"Do less and accomplish more. Do nothing and accomplish everything."
—Maharishi Mahesh Yogi

The Divine Revelation Breakthrough is not an experimental process. It is a field-proven method, tested throughout the world since the 1960s, when Peter Meyer first began teaching people how to hear the voice of God. I have personally facilitated the breakthrough experience for thousands of people.

You will benefit from the know-how that we have acquired by teaching so many people. As a result of our expertise, your experience will be easy, safe, gentle, enjoyable, and relaxing. The CD can help you open your heart and mind to the presence of God and experience your Divine Revelation Breakthrough Session in a simple, effortless, harmonious way.

Movement of Awareness

During your breakthrough session, you will be led through various levels of awareness step by step, until you experience the presence of God. Your conscious mind will travel from the level of the environment, to the physical level, then to the mental level, and eventually to the divine Spirit within.

Your conscious mind is a malleable entity, which can experience anything. For example, your mind senses your environment through sight, hearing, touch, taste, and smell. Also, your mind is aware of your body. You feel physical sensations such as pleasure and pain. Your mind is conscious of mental thoughts and visions. And your mind can experience the presence of God and other divine experiences through the subtle senses of clairvoyance, clairaudience, and clairsentience.

Your mind experiences the outer life during waking life, and the inner life during dreams and meditation. The phrase *Extra Sensory Perception* (ESP) is a misnomer, because you cannot experience anything without your senses. Your gross senses of seeing, hearing, tasting, smelling, and feeling experience the outer life. Your subtle senses of clairvoyance (subtle sight), clairaudience (subtle sound), clairsentience (subtle feeling), and clairgustance (subtle smell and taste) experience the inner life.

During your breakthrough, your mind will journey from the outer to the inner life, as illustrated in Figure 5a. You will experience your environment, body, mind, and Spirit. Then you travel beyond the spiritual world and transcend to absolute pure consciousness—eternal silence, peace, and perfection. That state of wholeness and one-ness is known as *samadhi, satori, nirvana,* or *satchitananda*—the Impersonal God.

Albert Marsh, a retired architect from Los Angeles describes his experience of the Impersonal God: *"During a process on your retreat in Mount Shasta, I experienced the pure void, the pure peace of mindlessness. It was my most profound experience I had ever had up to this moment. In this place of peace there is no thought, no movement, no desire, no emotion, no need for any action whatsoever. For want of a better*

Experiencing Dimensions of Your Self

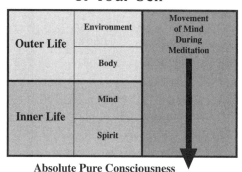

Absolute Pure Consciousness

Figure 5a

word, it is peace. Normally when I reach these realms, I weep with tears of love and gratitude, but even this didn't happen, I experienced a clear and totally empty, peaceful mind."

Elizabeth Wilson, an aesthetician from Westminster, California, reports: *"I experienced the awakened state at Mount Shasta, and it was as has been described by Buddha and others. No desire, no emotion, no need to take action, total emptiness, total peace, calm, love, beauty, all is perfect as it is right now. It's hard to put into words. That is the true reality."*

There are many levels of awareness, and, on your journey to inner space, you can visit all of them. Please refer to Figure 5b, which depicts a roadmap to your inner life. This chart represents both the outer life and the inner life.

Here are a few highlights of this chart:

Your mind is comprised of the conscious mind, subconscious mind, and façade barrier (ego)—an illusory veil that believes it is separate from God, isolated, and alone. This barrier is not real. The truth is that God is within you and all around you.

Your immortal soul is also known as etheric self, or *jiva*, which embodies your true heartfelt desires and divine purpose for this lifetime.

The Christ self or Christ consciousness is not "Christian." Rather, it is part of your higher self, no matter what your religion. Your Christ self reflects an ideal life, as the healer, the embodiment of unconditional love, forgiveness, redemption, peace, joy, and compassion.

Roadmap to Your Inner Life

Outer Life (Material World)	Body	Environment
		Physical Body
	Mind	Conscious Mind
		Subconscious Mind
		Façade Barrier (False Belief in Separation from God)
Inner Life (Spiritual World)		Etheric (Soul) Self
	Spirit	Christ Self
		"I AM" Self
		God Self
		Cosmic Self
Absolute Pure Consciousness (Present Everywhere)		

Figure 5b

Your "I AM" self, or *atman*, is the subtlest aspect of your individuality. On Mount Horeb, Moses saw an angel of the Lord appear as a burning bush. God called to Moses to demand that the Pharaoh of Egypt free the Israelites from slavery. When Moses asked God what he should say to Pharaoh, God replied, "I AM THAT I AM.... Thus shalt thou say unto the children of Israel, I AM hath sent me unto you."[1]

The mighty "I AM" presence is the essence of God, your higher self, your true spiritual nature of being. This is the embodiment of inner wisdom, truth, light, and enlightenment, the deepest level of your individuality.

Your God self is the devotional aspect of your being—the embodiment of pure love. You might experience it as streams of God's light and waves of God's love. Or you may see, feel, or hear God in whatever form you believe God to be.

Your cosmic self is a vast being—pervasive and immense as the universe. All the stars and galaxies, the entire cosmos is embodied within your cosmic self. Thus you might experience a limitless, expanded being, while your senses might expand to infinite sensitivity.

Absolute transcendental consciousness is beyond both the outer and inner life. It is unmanifest, eternal, unbounded, and infinite—beyond the mind and senses. You might experience it as deep peace, silence, perfection, expansion, oneness, and wholeness.

As an artist, I created an illustration that depicts these personal and universal aspects of God within you. Just above the human woman is her immortal, etheric soul-self, holding a bouquet of roses. Two robed figures flanking her represent her male and female Christ selves. Her male and female "I AM" selves hold a scroll with the Hebrew letters YOD HEH VAV HEH, meaning "I AM THAT I AM." Her male and female God selves are wearing crowns. The female figure just below the dove is the feminine aspect of God, the Holy Spirit. The stars and galaxies represent the cosmic self. The sun is the Impersonal God, shining its radiance everywhere.

These aspects of your higher self will be visited during your breakthrough session.

Figure 5c

For more details about these multidimensional levels of awareness, please read my books *Divine Revelation* and *Exploring Auras*.

Ken Krueger, a carpenter from Watertown, Wisconsin, describes: *"As I went through the façade layer and several of the other layers, my body had trembling sensations. Every spiritual level had a different feeling of love. I saw my infinite vision spinning and had a tone present that I never experienced before. The most profound experience was the power surge from the Holy Spirit. It felt like energy was entering every part of my body. The sensation was awesome."*

A real estate investor from Chicago, George Rawlings, describes: *"I saw a distinct picture of the cosmic self out in space, stars, a pulsating light."*

THE BREAKTHROUGH MEDITATION

The CD included with this book contains a guided meditation, recorded especially for this book to help you experience your breakthrough. This recording will lead you into meditation, step by step, as you listen to and follow my voice. An advantage of guided meditation is that no particular talent, skill, or training is required. Just follow the simple instructions on the CD. The entire session will be easy, effortless, safe, comfortable, enjoyable, and relaxing.

Many people have reported that, in Divine Revelation guided meditations, they have gone deeper into meditation than ever before:

Bette Margolis of Denver, shares: *"The meditation that you led the audience through was the most profound that I have ever experienced."*

"For the first time I'm able to feel inner peace. I feel light, lifted, and carefree," writes Patty Stern, a homemaker from Iowa City.

Charles Wright, a physician from Tampa, describes: *"My meditations were deeper than ever before. My understanding of the spiritual world expanded."*

Linda Vernon, a trucker from Brandon, Florida, reports: *"Much to my surprise, I was able to contact Spirit, get messages, and feel healing. I went to places within that I never even knew existed. My heart and soul were so deeply touched."*

During the meditation on the CD, I will begin with an opening prayer. You will say some affirmations to help you receive divine protection and achieve mental clarity. Then I will call upon God to lift your energy and the energy of your environment.

You will be led through various levels of awareness step by step, until you experience the presence of God. You will travel from the level of environment, to the physical level, through the mental level, reaching the divine Spirit. Then you will transcend beyond the spiritual world to absolute pure consciousness—the Impersonal God. You will experience that deep silence for a few moments.

Then I will call upon Holy Spirit to help you achieve four basic experiences: the Presence of God (inner contact), Name of God (inner name), Signal of God (inner signal or divine signal), and Message of God (inner message) from the Holy Spirit in female form. These four signposts are described in detail in Chapter 4. Please study that chapter before listening to the CD. There will be silent times during the meditation when you will receive the Signal of God and the Message of God.

When it is time to come out of meditation, you will take several deep breaths as you return from the level of Spirit, to the subconscious mind, to the conscious mind, to the physical body, and then to the environment. Then you will say an affirmation out loud that will help you achieve balance and integrate the experience into your life.

It is not necessary to remember these details, because this is a guided meditation, and all you need to do is listen to my voice and follow the instructions. I will guide you every step of the way.

ASKING A QUESTION

Before you listen to the CD, please formulate a question that you will ask the Holy Spirit during the meditation. I suggest that the question begin with one of the following phrases:

- "What is wise for me to do about…?"
- "What is highest wisdom to do about…?"
- "What is the wisest choice for me to make regarding…?"
- "Is it wise for me to…?"
- "Please show me…."
- "Please tell me…."
- "Please give me wisdom about…."
- "How can I accomplish…?"

Please do not ask any fortune-telling questions or questions about the future, such as those that include the following phrases:

- "Will I…?"
- "Will he…?"
- "Will she…?"

- "Will they...?"
- "Will...happen?"
- "What will happen...?"

Why do I recommend avoiding fortune-telling questions? Fortune-telling means predicting the future. Yet, can the future be predicted accurately? I believe you have free will and therefore create your own destiny. You can change your future anytime by changing your attitude, thoughts, emotions, and intentions. However, by asking fortune-telling questions, you demonstrate a belief that free will does not exist and the future is predetermined by "fate." Such a presumption is false. Your future is not written in stone or in the stars. You can change your mind anytime and thereby change your future.

"Mind is the master. What hasn't been created by thought does not exist."
—Ayya Kemma

"The mind is everything. What you think, you become."
—Lord Buddha

"The world we have created is a product of our thinking. It cannot be changed without changing our thinking."
—Albert Einstein

When you ask fortune-telling questions, something or someone will happily answer, but I assure you it will not be the voice of God. That is because asking predictive questions lowers your vibration and attracts lower energies.

Thus I recommend that you ask God for "highest wisdom." When you ask questions like, "What is wise for me to do about...?" then you demonstrate the belief that you have power to command your destiny by making wise decisions. God is always there to offer guidance and help you make purposeful choices. Therefore, please frame questions within the context of free will. To learn all the details about how to ask questions of God, please read *Divine Revelation*, especially Chapter 14.

Please take a moment now to formulate the question that you will ask during your breakthrough session. Write down your question so it is fixed in your mind. Make sure it is not a predictive or fortune-telling question.

Seven Rules for Asking Questions

1	Avoid predictive questions.
2	Only ask questions that assume free will.
3	Ask for "highest wisdom" rather than "should's."
4	Ask to be shown or taught rather than "have-to's."
5	Ask for divine guidance.
6	Ask clear and simple questions.
7	Ask only one question at a time.

Figure 5d

MEDITATION INSTRUCTIONS

During the meditation you will be instructed to take many deep breaths. Please breathe deeply. The deep breaths are essential to take you deep into the meditative state. Please breathe in through your nose. You may exhale through your nose or mouth, but please inhale only through the nose. (For an explanation about nose versus mouth breathing, please refer to *Exploring Chakras* and *Exploring Auras*.) When I ask you to take a deep breath, just take one deep breath—not several deep breaths and not hyperventilating. After you have taken that deep breath, then resume your normal breathing.

As you meditate, please listen to my voice and follow the instructions. This is the do-nothing program. That means do nothing, nothing, and less than nothing. Doing nothing means letting go and having a neutral attitude, not looking for a name, a signal, or a message, not seeking any particular experience. No effort, strain, or trying is allowed. No expectations are allowed.

Be comfortable as you meditate. Sit up in a comfortable chair, on a bed, or against some pillows on the floor, with back support. Please take any necessary bathroom breaks. If you need to move, stretch, scratch, or adjust yourself, please feel free to do so. Meditation is not strict, rigid, or uncomfortable. It is easy, effortless, and relaxing.

Let us begin. Make sure you are in a secure, cozy place indoors where you will not be disturbed for the next 70 minutes. Check the thermostat. People tend to get chilly during meditation. Turn off your phone and cell phone, and lock your door. If needed, place a note on your door: "Do Not Disturb." Place pets in another room. Make sure that children have supervision.

Now take out the CD and get into a comfortable seated position. Keep your remote control or control panel nearby, so that you can pause the recording anytime you feel the need for longer silent periods during the meditation. Play the CD at a low, soothing volume. When you are instructed on the CD to close your eyes, please keep your eyes closed until you are told to open them. Do the do-nothing program. Do nothing, nothing, and less than nothing. Please listen to the entire 70-minute CD.

"You need not leave your room. Remain sitting at your table and listen.
You need not even listen, simply wait, just learn to become quiet, still,
and solitary. The world will freely offer itself to you to be unmasked.
It has no choice; it will roll in ecstasy at your feet."
—Franz Kafka

"All of man's troubles stem from his inability to sit quietly in a room alone."
—Blaise Pascal

"In that one second when the human mind is still,
the experience of God comes."
—Joel Goldsmith

AFTER YOUR BREAKTHROUGH

After you come out of meditation, please take a moment to write down your inner name(s) and signal(s) that you received during your session. Figure 5e is a chart to help you remember your signals. Do not wait until "later" to make this record. It is vital to record this information immediately after you receive it.

Please use this chart as an ongoing register to log all your inner names and signals now and in the future. Then you can always refer back to this log to identify your inner divine contacts. Simply fill in each name, the sex of the divine being (for example, Mother Mary is female and Jesus is male), and describe its signal on the chart in Figure 5e.

Personal Divine Contacts

Inner Divine Names	Sex	Inner Divine Signals

Figure 5e

In addition to the CD, there are several other tools that might facilitate your breakthrough experience:

1. Take a private Divine Revelation Breakthrough Session with me on the telephone.

2. Attend one of my spiritual retreats, which I hold regularly in various spiritual vortexes.

3. Look at my itinerary on my Website and attend one of my workshops or classes.

4. Join my mailing list on my Website to be notified of workshops, classes, retreats, teleseminars, and Webinars.

5. Order a video or audio seminar through my Website. These were recorded live at my experiential seminars.

6. Find a teacher in your area, listed on my Website.

7. Invite me to come to your area. You will be compensated for sponsoring me, plus you will get to take the seminar for free.

8. Visit my Website for more information: *www.divinerevelation.org*.

How to Meditate on Your Own

One way to verify your inner names and signals is to take a workshop or session from a qualified teacher. However, you can identify your own inner names and signals, and receive inner messages with a simple meditation: Just sit down; close your eyes; take a few deep breaths; get quiet, comfortable, still, balanced, and centered; and then ASK.

ASKING is the key. In fact, the entire Divine Revelation methodology is based on a single principle: "Ask, and it shall be given you."[2] By asking, you receive the signal. By asking, you receive the inner name, the healing, the blessing, and the answer to your questions. Just ASK.

What follows is a meditation to help you receive inner divine names, signals, and messages. Before attempting this, please study the remainder of this book and learn how to use the 10 Tests of Spiritual Discernment.

1. Begin With a Prayer.

Speak aloud a prayer, such as: *"I recognize that there is one power and presence in the universe, God the good, omnipotent. I am one with this power and presence of God. Therefore, I claim my perfect divine signal and divine message to come to me now with divine order and timing. I call upon (name of an aspect of God) to give me a divine signal and message. I release any seeming blockages that have prevented me from receiving my perfect divine signal and message now. I release and let go of all ideas that I am separate from God or that God is out of reach. I accept and welcome with open arms my perfect divine contact with God now. Thank you, God, and SO IT IS."*

In the blank space, place the name of an aspect of God that you like and that you feel comfortable with. The "Name of God" was explained on page 46 of this book.

2. Take a Few Deep Breaths.

Take breaths into your body very deeply. Fill your whole body with breath. Deep breathing is essential to help you get your signal and message. Inhale and exhale slowly until you feel relaxed, centered, and balanced.

With every deep breath, imagine, as you exhale, that you are sinking out of your head and into your heart. Just pretend you are sinking into your heart. Take several deep breaths like this until you feel relaxed. Then resume your normal breathing.

3. Relax Your Body.

Say out loud: *"I now let go of the outer environment and go deeper to the physical level."* Become aware of your body. Notice any tension, pain, or other sensations, and quietly place your attention there, until you feel the sensations dissipate. If you like, you can imagine relaxing each part of your body progressively, starting at your toes and feet, and going up to your scalp. Take more deep breaths. Sink out of your head and into your heart as you exhale and go deeper.

4. Relax Your Conscious Mind.

Say out loud: *"I now relax and become aware of my conscious mind."* Bring your attention to your mind. Imagine that your mind is quiet and still, like a still pond without a ripple, or like a candle flame that does not waver. Take more deep breaths and go deeper. Sink out of your head and into your heart as you let go of each deep breath.

5. Relax Your Subconscious Mind.

Say out loud: *"I now relax to the level of my subconscious mind."* Become aware of your subconscious mind. Enter a deep state of relaxation as you connect with deeper levels of mind, which are below surface thoughts and emotions. Take more deep breaths and relax more deeply. Sink out of your head and into your heart as you let go of each breath, until you feel connected with Spirit.

6. Connect With God.

Surrender to the loving presence of God, in a state of oneness and wholeness—deeply relaxed, expanded, and filled with perfect peace and bliss. If you are not in that state, then continue deep breathing, or use the appropriate healing prayers in Chapter 7 of this book.

7. Ask for Your Signal.

Say out loud: *"I call upon (name of an aspect of God) to give me your divine signal now. Feed it stronger, feed it stronger, feed it stronger."*

8. Let Go and Let God.

Take another deep breath. Do nothing and less than nothing. Do not look for anything or try to get a signal. Just have a neutral attitude in a state of beingness. That means let go and let God do it. This is the "do-nothing" program. Give up completely. Do absolutely nothing.

9. Recognize and Verify Your Signal.

You will see, hear, taste, smell, or feel something, or get a body movement. That will, most likely, be your signal. If you are not getting a clear signal, then go back to number 2 and repeat the procedure.

Once you recognize a clear signal, then say something like the following aloud: "(*name of an aspect of God*), *if the signal that I identify as being* (*describe the signal*) *is your signal, then please feed it stronger to me now.*" You will notice your signal getting stronger when you ask the aspect of God to feed it stronger. If it diminishes or disappears, then go back to number 2 and repeat the same procedure.

10. Ask for Your Message.

Say something like the following aloud: "(*name of an aspect of God*), *please tell me* (*your question or request*) *now.*" Ask questions and have a conversation with your higher self. It is necessary to ASK. Otherwise, God will not respond.

11. Let Go and Let God.

Take another big deep breath. Do nothing and less than nothing. Do not try to get a message. Just have a neutral attitude and give up completely. Be receptive. You might think you are just making up the answers, and, in a sense, you are, because you are that divine presence within you, and your higher self is answering your questions. Trust in what you receive.

12. Give Gratitude and Return.

Slowly come out of meditation. Take a deep breath and blow it out, as if you were blowing out a candle. Say something like, "*I now thank God for this wonderful meditation and for all that I have received.*" (Blow out a candle.) "*I now return from the level of Spirit to the level of subconscious mind, knowing that my subconscious mind has been healed by this meditation.*" (Blow out a candle.) "*I now return to the level of conscious mind, knowing that my conscious mind is one with the mind of God.*" (Blow out a candle.) "*I now return to the level of physical body, knowing that my body is in perfect health.*" (Blow out a candle.) "*I now come back to the level of the environment, bringing back with me all the blessings I have received in this meditation.*"

Then blow out four more candles and come all the way back to inner and outer balance. Then say out loud in a clear voice, "*I AM alert. I AM awake. I AM inwardly and outwardly balanced. I AM divinely protected by the light of my being. Thank you, God, and SO IT IS.*"

13. Difficulties?

If you have difficulty using this procedure, then you can:

1. Meditate with the enclosed CD again to help you receive signals and messages.

2. Read the rest of this book and study the 10 tests.

3. Read *Divine Revelation* and use the meditation procedure in Chapter 8 and the healing prayers in Chapter 10.

4. Contact a qualified Divine Revelation teacher and make an appointment to verify your inner names and signals. For a list

of qualified teachers and more information, go to *www.divinerevelation.org*.

YOUR HOMEWORK ASSIGNMENTS

After you have received a signal and message from the Holy Spirit by using the enclosed CD, it is vital to continue to use this signal in daily meditation. Your homework assignment is to meditate with your inner contact daily for at least the next 30 days. You can meditate for five minutes or for 50 minutes, depending on how much time is available that day.

The 70-minute guided meditation on the CD included with this book is too long for most people to use daily. Therefore, I offer a guided meditation CD on *www.divinerevelation.org* to help you practice hearing the voice of God on a daily basis. Or you can record your own CD or audiotape by following the instructions in Chapter 8 of *Divine Revelation* or Chapter 5 of *Exploring Meditation*.

In addition to daily meditation, your homework assignment is to call upon an aspect of God, such as Holy Spirit or another inner name, at least three times a day for at least 30 days. Ask for love, healing, lifting, spiritual experiences, answers to questions, or inspiration. At the end of 30 days, send an e-mail to divinerev@aol.com, or write a letter to Susan Shumsky, Divine Revelation, P.O. Box 7185, New York, NY 10116, to report your results. Write at least two paragraphs describing your inner names, signals, messages, and spiritual experiences that you receive.

Stuart Van Niekerk, an English teacher from Scotland, says: *"I think that what is important is the Breakthrough. It is about discovering your own, personal revelations from within. We know that we are just the vessels of whatever comes through, and weigh each tidbit of information carefully against our own inner guidance. You can show me the truth, but unless I know it and understand it from within, then I am still blind. 'Open the eyes of my heart, Lord.'"*[3]

⟜

In Part III you will learn how to get clear messages from the divine voice, and how to distinguish between the true divine voice and other voices in your mind.

~ PART III ~

PRACTICING SAFE SPIRITUALITY

Chapter 6

ALL THAT GLITTERS IS NOT GOD

"Do not follow the ideas of others, but learn to listen to the voice within yourself. Your body and mind will become clear and you will realize the unity of all things."

—Dôgen Zenji

You can talk to God—and God will talk back. Yet, how do you know it is really God? Could someone or something be disguised as God? How can you identify a divine experience when you have one? How would you determine whether the message is real?

These are the kinds of questions that anyone who seeks to hear the voice of God asks. To realize what God feels like, you must recognize how the divine realm differs from other planes of reality (or unreality). As you open to inner sensing, it is easy to delude yourself that you are contacting the true voice of God, when you are not.

BECOMING SPIRITUALLY STREET-SMART

In order for you to receive clear, precise divine messages, it is important to attain spiritual discernment. Here you will learn to distinguish between the true voice of Spirit and other voices in your mind. You will begin to ascertain whether your inner guidance is the real thing.

Right now it is popular to develop psychic abilities. Many people contact their "guides," talk to "angels," get messages from "departed spirits," become a "channeler," or communicate with the "dead." With the popularity of John Edwards, James Van Praagh, Sylvia Browne, Lisa Williams, and others, it is chic to be a medium.

Those who seek spiritual guidance are now opening to invisible realms. Yet, some people access the unseen world by blindly communicating with whatever happens to be floating by. Would you open your door to a stranger and invite him to take over your home? This is analogous to opening to "guides" without knowing who or what you are contacting.

What does it mean to be "spiritually street-smart"? You are undoubtedly street-wise as you walk down the street. You carefully watch your possessions while riding the city bus or subway. Yet many people are not so street-smart when entering the inner realms. They dive into a dark, choppy ocean, filled with dangerous riptides, without first learning how to swim. With this book, you will master swimming before diving into a deep ocean.

You are street-wise in your outer life. Now is the time to become street-wise in your inner life. You need spiritual street-smarts to discern the genuine voice of God from other voices that may try to deceive you. These voices can jump in anytime and interrupt God's true voice. Therefore, it is essential to "practice safe spirituality."

TUNING INTO THE GOD STATION

Hearing the voice of God is like tuning into a car radio. Some stations are clear, while others are distorted by static. Your goal is to determine which station to tune into and then to receive the signal clearly. The station broadcasting the message of God is called the realm of Spirit, spiritual realm, spiritual world, or spiritual plane. However, there are three other stations on your radio dial. Each message will arise from one of four dimensions or realms: (1) the spiritual world, (2) the mental world, (3) the astral world, or (4) the environment.

No matter which way you perceive the message, whether through clairvoyance, clairaudience, clairsentience, dreams, or any other way, every message comes from one of these four places. So, it is wise to discern: Where is this information coming from? Is it real? Who is the messenger? Is it my ego? Is it wishful thinking, or some other voice? Am I being hoodwinked?

Where Messages Come From

1	**SPIRITUAL WORLD**	**Voice of God**
2	**MENTAL WORLD**	**Internal Influences**
3	**ASTRAL WORLD**	**Lower Beings**
4	**ENVIRONMENT**	**External Influences**

Figure 6a

1. SPIRITUAL WORLD

The spiritual world is one of the dimensions that you might receive messages from. The true spiritual plane, also known as the celestial or heavenly world, is a realm of divine love, light, wholeness, oneness, peace, tranquility, joy, and fulfillment.

You visit this place whenever you feel inspired or close to God. Then you feel loved, protected, nurtured, calm, satisfied, happy, and free. God gives you a sense of faith, strength, wisdom, and beauty. You are illumined, blessed, enlightened, awakened, energized, elevated, motivated, assured, and confident, filled with well-being and divine grace. Unbounded awareness and expansiveness pervade you. The true realm of Spirit brings wonderment, awe, exaltation, unity, harmony, balance, centeredness, and contentment.

Most people believe they cannot visit this realm until they are dead. However, many people who practice meditation or prayer experience it on a daily basis. Here are some beings in this heavenly realm that you might encounter and communicate with:

- **God, Goddess, Father God, Mother God:** The God or Goddess that you believe in.

- **Deities**: The deity or deities of your religious or spiritual beliefs.
- **Divine Beings**: Sacred presences that live in the spiritual plane.
- **Angels, Archangels**: Messengers of God. Archangels are the highest rank of angels.
- **Guardian Angels**: Messengers of God that protect and guide human beings.
- **Saints, Prophets, Sages**: Enlightened beings who have attained a higher level of consciousness.
- **Ascended Masters**: Enlightened beings who transformed their physical bodies into light and moved into the spiritual plane, leaving no physical body behind. As immortal beings, they can travel at the speed of thought and can manifest a body and appear anytime to anyone.
- **Your Higher Self**: The aspect of yourself that is perfect, complete, whole, and one with God. You are a multidimensional being, and you have both a lower and higher self. The lower self is your ego, and the higher self is your Christ Self, "I AM" Self, and God Self.
- **Christ Consciousness**: Your Christ Self, or the aspect of yourself that is pure love, healing, joy, and compassion.
- **Departed Loved Ones in the Divine Light**: Those beloved souls who were your loved ones when alive and then, after death, moved into the divine light and now live in the spiritual plane or "heaven." Once they move into the light, they can become spiritual beings, divine teachers, or guardians. Therefore, it is safe to contact and receive messages from them.

I highly recommend that you receive all your messages and inner experiences from the spiritual plane. In this book you are learning to get messages from this divine world, rather than other levels of existence.

2. MENTAL WORLD

The mental realm is the second area of existence that you might tap into when receiving messages. This plane includes your sensory mind, subconscious mind, and emotional mind.

Sensory Mind

Your sensory mind, also known as lower mind, is the aspect of mind that experiences life through the senses. It is characterized by incessant patter, like a chat room that is always online and never shuts down. Some self-talk is encouraging and positive; however, by the time the average person is an adult, millions of negative messages have poisoned the mind at a much higher rate than positive messages have elevated it.

Most of your nonstop mind-talk is about your everyday activities: "I have to pick up the kids at 4:00," "I'm late for work," "I've got to get some milk on the way home," or "I'm exhausted and want to go to bed." These thoughts, on the mental plane, are ordinary thoughts about daily life. Rarely does anyone ever transcend this realm of lower mind.

However, there are times when you are touched by Spirit, and ordinary thoughts take an extraordinary turn. These are times of great insight and inspiration, when you attune to the spiritual realm rather than the mental world. Have you ever said something uncharacteristically profound and then thought, "Who said that? Where did that insight come from?" In such instances, you have tapped into your higher mind, the mind of God.

The lower mind does not supply such serendipitous events. It is where thought drones in accustomed grooves. No magic occurs there—no new insights or meaningful wisdom. It is simply a humdrum rehash of banal old tapes, playing over and over, quite unconsciously.

Subconscious Mind

Your subconscious mind is a repository of everything you have ever experienced throughout your lifetimes. It behaves like a computer hard drive, storing memory imprints of every sensory input. Everything you have ever learned, all the books you have read, teachers you have encountered, experiences you have had—all are kept there. This includes all conditioned habits, ideas, and concepts that you have been brainwashed to believe—from parents, teachers, society, peers, the media, and so on. Such repetitive entrainment results in crystallized habits and tendencies that seem difficult to change.

Emotional Mind

Positive emotions are a bridge between your thoughts and the spiritual world. Emotions such as love, elation, and joy indicate that the spiritual realm is near. However, negative emotions suggest that you are far from the spiritual plane.

Your negative emotions could be perceived consciously or experienced unconsciously. Some of these are anger, hostility, hate, fear, frustration, anxiety, worry, timidity, guilt, resentment, sadness, shame, dejection, confusion, illness, obsession, conceitedness, criticism, exhaustion, depression, jealousy, possessiveness, selfishness, confusion, impatience, and others.

If you are having negative emotions or a flat, hollow, empty experience, then you are in the mental world rather than touching the feet of God.

Thus, the mental world contains:

- **Habits, Patterning**: Deep repetitious behaviors that are often unconscious.

- **Conditioning**: Learned behaviors and tendencies that arise from repetitious control, indoctrination, or influence from an external source.

- **Thought Forms**: Beliefs, concepts, ideas, or constructs so intense that they crystallize into subtle form to comprise a subtle body called the "mental body."

- **Memories**: Past knowledge, experiences, and sensory experiences retained in your unconscious or conscious mind.

- **Experience Imprints**: The retention of impressions of everything that has ever happened to you, in this life and past lives.

- **Belief Systems**: A collection of ideas or "-isms" that you have accepted as truth. Sometimes called "B.S.," they are often false assumptions and erroneous constructs.

- **Mental Law**: The established group of limited beliefs, often bound by egotistical needs and delusions, that you have allowed to determine what happens in your life.

- **Past Influences**: Beliefs you have accepted from parents, teachers, friends, religious training, or past relationships. Influences from your past can haunt you.

Holding such negative attitudes will prevent you from hearing the voice of God. As a coach named Jim Ward says, *"If you look in the rearview mirror for too long, you will crash."*

As you open to inner messages, you might inadvertently contact the mental world and delude yourself into thinking that these are true divine messages, when, in fact, you are just talking to yourself. So-called "revelations" might actually be past memories, fantasies, wishful thinking, or messages concocted in lower mind. You might be unconsciously recalling something you read 10 years ago that you subsequently forgot about. Or you may be regurgitating erroneous beliefs instilled by societal brainwashing. It is easy to believe that God is speaking to you, when it is, instead, all in your mind.

Sadly, most so-called "channeled" books are received from the mental world—not the spiritual realm. Many sincere authors think their messages come from a spiritual source, but they are mistaken. Sometimes, at least in the beginning, these authors were receiving true divine revelations, but their own unconscious mind distorted the message.

How the Mind Distorts God's Message

LEVELS OF AWARENESS:	HOW MESSAGE IS GIVEN:		
	VISUAL	AUDITORY	KINESTHETIC
God Spiritual Body	**Divine Messages:** Revelations, Inspirations		
Feeling Mind Emotional Body	Images	Ideas	Feelings
Façade Mind Façade Body	Subconscious Filter: Mankind adds fear to God's Message		
Conscious Mind Mental Body	Visions	Thoughts	Sensations

Figure 6b

Figure 6b illustrates how the mind distorts the true message of God. Revelations and inspirational messages are fed directly from God as visual (seeing), auditory (hearing), or kinesthetic (feeling) experiences.

The first filter to receive the pure message of God is the feeling mind, which perceives it as images, ideas, or feelings. The message then travels to the façade body, also known as ego—the aspect of mind that, according to the ascended master Mahavatar Babaji, "adds fear to God's message." The façade mind, which clings to false, egoic concepts of separation from God, might skew God's message, add to it, or subtract from it. Finally, the distorted message appears to the conscious mind, and the recipient consciously perceives it as visions, thoughts, or sensations.

Your mind can easily be deceived. If you are not deep enough or clear enough to receive the true divine message, then it will be distorted. In this book you are learning to go deep into meditation and heal false beliefs, allowing you to receive accurate inner guidance and clear messages from God.

Make sure you are contacting the true spiritual world rather than the mental realm. Trust your deepest feelings. A sense of wholeness, oneness, contentment, happiness, and energy are unmistakable signs of God.

3. Astral World

The astral realm is the third plane of existence that you might receive messages from. It is sometimes called limbo or purgatory. Beings that are not in physical bodily form, yet are not on the spiritual plane, inhabit this invisible, discordant dimension. These beings live in a gray, confined, joyless place of sorrow, ignorance, and illusion.

Some astral beings are humans who died, yet, for any number of reasons, did not move on. Others are beings that have never taken human embodiment, yet choose to dwell in this murky habitation. Misleading, false messages and physically draining and psychologically damaging experiences may arise from contacting such beings.

Near-Death Experiences

You may have heard about the *near death-experience*, or NDE. Survivors of the NDE experienced temporary death. Their electrocardiogram (EKG) registered what is known as *flatline*. The medical term is *asystole* (no heartbeat, no respiration, and temporary brain death). According to near-death researchers such as Raymond Moody, author of *Life After Life*, specific phenomena commonly occur when a person visits the afterlife, then lives to tell the tale.

Most near-death survivors first encounter a tunnel, road, highway, or opening. They meet dead relatives or close friends, who usher them toward a brilliant light of immeasurable glory. On the way, they see other beings that are grayer or slower and not in the light. When they move into the light, they meet a luminous being, which they might identify as a deity. Many NDE survivors report seeing Jesus, their own higher self, or an angel.

Some NDE survivors claim to experience a 360-degree panoramic "life review," in which their entire life flashes before them. Some of them see this from not only their own viewpoint, but also the standpoint of every person they have ever encountered. The survivor stands in the shoes of each person, and experiences firsthand how the survivor's actions affected that person.

I believe that NDE survivors have had genuine afterlife experiences, and they describe exactly what happens after death. However, some souls, for a variety of reasons, do not move into the light after death. Instead, they get stuck or stranded in the astral world. Who or what lives in this world? Here are some beings that dwell there:

- **Discarnate Entities:** Beings who are not in physical form. They dwell in the gray world of the astral plane.
- **Earthbound Spirits:** Departed souls who did not move into the spiritual world after death. They remain stuck in materialistic awareness as confused, lost souls.
- **Classes of Spirits:** Several classes of entities dwell in the astral world, whether or not they have ever taken human form. Alan Kardec, famed Spiritualist and author of *The Spirits Book*,[1] has delineated 10 classes of spirits in three orders: Imperfect Spirits, Good Spirits, and Pure Spirits:

Kardec's Classes of Spirits

FIRST ORDER: Pure Spirits	Class 1 →	Pure Spirits
	Class 2 →	High Spirits
SECOND ORDER: Good Spirits	Class 3 →	Wise Spirits
	Class 4 →	Learned Spirits
	Class 5 →	Benevolent Spirits
	Class 6 →	Noisy Spirits
	Class 7 →	Neutral Spirits
THIRD ORDER: Imperfect Spirits	Class 8 →	Pretentious Spirits
	Class 9 →	Frivolous Spirits
	Class 10 →	Impure Spirits

Figure 6c

Third Order—Imperfect Spirits: This order of spirits is entirely materialistic, with cruel, malicious intentions:

> **Impure Spirits** ("**Saboteurs**") include demons, evil genii, or evil spirits. Entirely malevolent, they retard humans' spiritual advancement, and take pleasure in convincing humans to harm themselves or others.
>
> **Frivolous Spirits** ("**Mischievous**") may be ghosts, hobgoblins, will-o'-the-wisps, pixies, sprites, fairies, or gnomes—meddling beings that enjoy misleading humans with false hopes and trickery.
>
> **Pretentious Spirits** ("**Fakers**") seduce naïve humans with false promises of secret, elite, occult mysteries or scientific knowledge. Pompous and arrogant, they feign special powers and "high" consciousness. Alluring messages that denote an air of gravity are carefully calculated to impress the susceptible. Faker spirits, frustrated and craving attention, hanker for ego glorification. They cling to living human mediums willing to impart their "message." Many best-selling channeled books are written by fakers, seeking fame, glamour, and glory.
>
> **Neutral Spirits** are earthbound spirits, strongly attached to the pleasures, desires, and regrets of earthly life. They neither help nor harm humans.
>
> **Noisy Spirits** are bound tightly to the material world. The German word *poltergeist* consists of roots *geist*, meaning "ghost," and *polter*, meaning "mischievous." Poltergeists are boisterous spirits that generate physical phenomena. They rattle windows, switch lights on and off, move furniture and other objects, close or open doors, and so on.

Second Order—Good Spirits: This order of spirits includes good genii, protecting genii, and good spirits. In times of ignorant superstition, they are regarded as benevolent deities. However, they retain human traits, such as eccentricities and hobbies. Though possessed of limited skills, they attempt to be helpful to humans. But they are only as useful, helpful, or truthful as they were when alive.

First Order—Pure Spirits: These perfected beings live in the spiritual world, rather than the astral realm. They dwell in the presence of God eternally and speak with the voice of God. They are messengers or ministers of God. They never incarnate in perishable bodies, though they can materialize any form. They might be divine beings, ascended masters, angels, archangels, and seraphim. Executors of God's orders, they maintain universal harmony, radiate pure love, and protect and assist humans. However, they never intrude or interfere in human affairs unless asked. Contacting Pure Spirits produces a 100 percent beneficial effect.

IMPORTANT: Receive your messages only from First Order—
Pure Spirits. Other messengers live in the astral world. Their
influence is not 100 percent positive. Rather, there would be a
mixture of beneficial and unbeneficial effects.

Why Souls Become Earthbound

After death, people have a choice. They can either enter the light, or else
wander aimlessly on the astral plane, confused, vulnerable, and powerless.
Such souls need help, and you can heal them with the Astral-Entity Healing
Affirmation on page 104. Without help, they might remain lost a long time,
even centuries.

Why Souls Become Earthbound

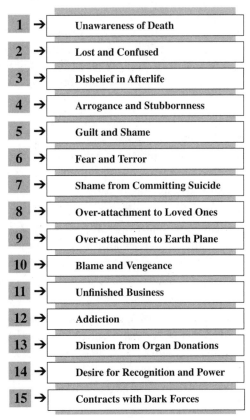

1 →	Unawareness of Death
2 →	Lost and Confused
3 →	Disbelief in Afterlife
4 →	Arrogance and Stubbornness
5 →	Guilt and Shame
6 →	Fear and Terror
7 →	Shame from Committing Suicide
8 →	Over-attachment to Loved Ones
9 →	Over-attachment to Earth Plane
10 →	Blame and Vengeance
11 →	Unfinished Business
12 →	Addiction
13 →	Disunion from Organ Donations
14 →	Desire for Recognition and Power
15 →	Contracts with Dark Forces

Figure 6d

Why would a soul not cross over into the divine light after death? In Figure 6d, there are 15 reasons:

1. **Unawareness of Death:** Perhaps a person's death is unexpected, accidental, or violent. The soul catapults from its body without realizing it is dead. This happens because, at death, the mind separates from the body. Thus, it continues entirely conscious, thinking thoughts, feeling emotions, and using the senses. Yet the mind expects to change or disappear at death. So, although the mind has an expectation of death, it continues to function as if alive. In other words, there is no death, but humans expect death. Thus, they believe they are still alive.

2. **Lost and Confused:** The soul might be lost, confused, and wandering in the astral plane in a dazed state. Some causes might be Alzheimer's disease, senility, or taking heavy drugs just before death.

3. **Disbelief in Afterlife:** Perhaps the individual does not believe in God, a light, or an afterlife. Convinced that nothing exists after death, the soul does not see or enter the light. However, the fact is that with just one thought of God, the divine light will appear.

4. **Arrogance and Stubbornness:** NDE survivors report meeting departed loved ones in the tunnel who are pointing the way, ushering them into the light. However, if people are arrogant or stubborn, then, after death, they might not accept help from loved ones in the tunnel.

5. **Guilt and Shame:** Some people are convinced and constantly reinforced about how sinful they are. In such cases, filled with shame and guilt, the departed soul may feel unworthy to enter the divine light. This is a sad state when their heartfelt desire to go to heaven has been squelched by the very religion they have followed with such fervor.

6. **Fear and Terror:** Some people believe they will enter the "Pearly Gates" and meet Saint Peter at death. Then, the big book will appear, and their sins will be revealed. As a result of this "judgment day," the soul believes it will be condemned to hellfire and damnation. Anticipation of such terror can prevent a soul from moving into the light.

7. **Shame from Committing Suicide:** People who commit suicide might be seized by shame and guilt. Such shame will prevent

them from moving into the divine light. However, even suicide victims can enter the light after death. But they have a unique type of life review. They see what their life would have been, had they continued to live.

8. **Over-attachment to Loved Ones:** The soul might be overly attached to loved ones remaining on earth. Or living relatives are overly attached to the departed soul and are holding it back. The purpose of the funeral is to help the soul move on. But loved ones can prevent it from crossing over into the divine light.

9. **Over-attachment to the Earth Plane:** The soul might be overly attached to the earth plane or material things. If such a soul obsesses about its home or workplace, or hungers for its possessions or pleasures, then it might continue to haunt a place, person, or building.

10. **Blame and Vengeance:** The soul may be angry, blaming, and seeking vengeance. Deceased souls cannot enter the light unless they are at peace. There is no peace for a soul that is clinging to anger and seeking revenge.

11. **Unfinished Business:** The soul might believe that it has unfinished business to accomplish before it is ready to move on. Perhaps the soul thinks its life was snatched away before the proper time, or that it needs to complete a specific task.

12. **Addiction:** Without a body, people addicted to substances cannot continue their habit after death. So, the soul might attach to a susceptible living human in order to continue enjoying pleasures of the flesh. The possessed person might suddenly undergo a personality change and become an addict. To learn more about astral oppression or possession, please read *Divine Revelation*. I also recommend Edith Fiore's *The Unquiet Dead*.

13. **Disunion from Organ Donations:** Individuals who perceive themselves as spiritual beings temporarily inhabiting a physical shell may donate organs and happily enter the light after death. However, a deceased soul that is overly attached to its physical body may feel terrorized when the body is dismembered. This will prevent the soul from moving on.

14. **Desire for Recognition and Power:** Certain people may be frustrated while chasing fame, recognition, and power. Then, in the afterlife, they might attach to vulnerable psychics, meditators,

mediums, or channelers. Using an impressive-sounding name, such as a biblical name, they achieve celebrity through their host.

Such faker spirits can hoodwink susceptible people with counterfeit "spiritual" experiences or complicated "high" messages. They are particularly dangerous, because they manipulate through flattery and other underhanded tactics as they convincingly masquerade as spiritual messengers.

15. **Contracts with Dark Forces:** The soul might believe it made a contract, pact, or agreement with dark forces and therefore thinks it cannot move into the light. However, such a Faustian myth is not real. Any soul may choose the light at any time.

How the Astral Plane Feels

How can you tell whether you are in contact with astral entities or true spiritual beings? You will know by how you feel. On the spiritual plane, you are elevated and filled with love, light, wholeness, peace, and joy. In contrast, the astral realm is a place of contraction, darkness, sadness, depression, emptiness, and fear. Astral entities cannot fake genuine spiritual experiences, because they are not spiritual. They cannot lift you to a higher plane than the one where they live.

Here is how Keith Cutrona, an advertising executive from Evanston, Illinois, described his Divine Revelation Breakthrough Session: *"It untangled the confusion between being possessed by spirits versus communication with the divine. I experienced greater certainty in my communication with God, like clearing the cobwebs. It is a reclaiming of what is lost. It's remarkable how strong and certain I feel."*

A nutritionist named Anne Campbell from Newport Beach, California, wrote about her breakthrough: *"I released impurities and disengaged connections from those beings who were other than the purity of God's love. Thank you for this."*

A Note About Departed Loved Ones

Do not confuse your departed loved ones with astral entities. Whereas entities are lost souls, your relatives are probably in the spiritual realm. To contact loved ones, be sure to use the 10 tests in Chapter 8. Faker spirits could pretend to be your beloved departed. In some cases, the souls of your relatives might be stranded in the astral plane and need healing. Heal them with the Astral-Entity Healing Affirmation on page 104 of this book.

Here is an example of a genuine spiritual contact with a departed loved one:

Arvin had been battling AIDS for several years, and, although he fought the good fight, he was nearing his time to depart. He was living in a hospice during his final days. One night at 3 a.m., Arvin's close friend Matthew bolted upright in his bed. He recognized Arvin's voice speaking to him in an undeniable, audible, clear way, "I implore you to wake up and follow life! I implore you to wake up and follow life! See me everywhere, in the flowers, in the raindrops, and most of all, in the smiles of the children." Arvin died, but his message transformed Matthew's life and has continued to be his guiding light and daily inspiration until this day. Matthew's willful nature has been tempered and softened, and he now has an appreciation for the little things in life.

———

By opening indiscriminately to inner messages without safeguards or tests, and without a roadmap to your inner life, you might be opening to danger. You could inadvertently tap into the astral world and delude yourself into thinking you are receiving genuine spiritual experiences. Thus, you might be tricked by astral entities.

Therefore, it is recommended that, along with your intuitive explorations, you regularly practice a form of spiritual discipline, such as prayer or meditation, so you can easily recognize the oneness, harmony, and wholeness of Spirit. You will then accurately identify the uncomfortable feelings that accompany astral influence.

4. Environment

The environment is the fourth realm from which you might receive messages. In other words, messages might arise from an external source, such as thoughts, feelings, emotions, or the physical presence of others. You could access vibrations of your surroundings, or pick up random flotsam and jetsam thought-forms that continually fluctuate in the mental atmosphere. Or you could tap the collective mind of humanity—everything that human beings believe as a whole. Here are a few examples of receiving messages from the environment:

- **Mind-Reading:** Talented psychics can read thought-forms in the mental body of their clients and thereby foretell the future, often accurately. That is because your future is already written in your thoughts—the seeds of future outcomes. Yet no psychic is 100 percent accurate. Changing your mind changes your future. Thus, mind-reading is not flawless. Read more about how you create your destiny in my book *Miracle Prayer*.
- **Environ-Mental Static:** In a crowded place, such as a football stadium or subway, or a place with a low vibration, such as a bar,

prison, or mental health institution, you might sense negative atmospheric mental conditions. Environ-mental static is negative energies in your surroundings that have a draining effect.

- **External Influences**: Your mind might be negatively affected by loved ones, co-workers, teachers, peers, clergy, or other people or things in your surroundings. You might be subject to peer pressure, constant coercion, or intimidation at home or work.

- **Religious Brainwashing**: You might be brainwashed by strongly held beliefs imposed by a religious institution. You may think that only an elite clergy is worthy to receive direct divine communication. The belief in an anthropomorphic God of anger and vengeance, including threats of afterlife horrors, is particularly toxic.

- **Societal Brainwashing**: The collective beliefs of civilization might deeply influence your mind. Examples might be "men are superior to women," or "rich people cannot be spiritual or religious."

- **Media Hype**: Poison beliefs are imposed upon people through print, television, radio, or Internet advertising. Examples of these beliefs include "youth is valuable and old age is useless," or "only lean, muscular people are sexually attractive."

- **Race-Mind Consciousness or Collective Unconscious**: Race-mind means the collective subconscious mind of the entire human race—the erroneous beliefs commonly agreed upon by humanity. This term has nothing to do with racial groups or skin color.

- **History of Humanity**: All memories, experiences, thoughts, words, and deeds that have ever occurred are recorded indelibly and held in collective consciousness. This *"akashic record"* is a history book that can be read by those capable of tapping into it, such as talented clairvoyants, who can see past lives or the record of ancient civilizations.

All of these environmental influences can hamper your ability to receive clear messages from God. Our planet is covered by an illusory astral cloud of negative beliefs, thought-forms, environ-mental static, and other dense mental material that impedes clear reception of divine experiences.

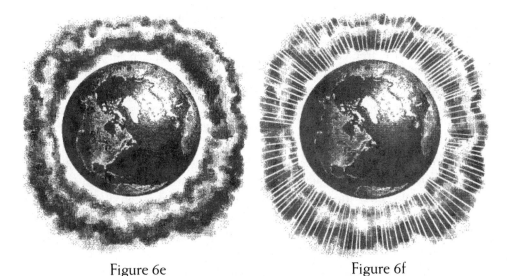

Figure 6e   Figure 6f

For the past 50 years, since light-workers have been diligently meditating, praying, healing, and engaging in other spiritual practices, this cloud has lifted significantly. Yet, a blinding astral haze still prevents many people from even imagining that God could speak to them directly.

You might inadvertently open up to this illusory astral cloud and think you are in contact with a divine voice. Instead, you are tapping the toxic refuse of environ-mental flotsam and jetsam that happens to be drifting by. You may read minds or the collective mind of humanity and believe you are receiving profound spiritual insights. You might impress your clients with your readings, but God is not impressed.

USING DISCERNMENT

We have just explored the four planes of existence that you might tap into when attempting to hear the voice of God: the spiritual, mental, astral, and environmental realms. Considering all the false detours you might take when exploring inner space, isn't it wise to get a roadmap to direct your pathway? There are many pitfalls on the path to inner guidance.

How can you differentiate between an astral entity, your mind, and the true voice of God? Not only will God answer your question with wisdom, but it will also give you comfort, joy, wisdom, serenity, inspiration, and vibrational lifting. The other three realms do not provide that illumined feeling of divine grace. God does not just provide information, so if you are solely receiving data without accompanying divine feelings, then you are not in contact with God.

Open to the true voice of Spirit. That is the message to trust. When you seek knowledge that is hidden from view, yet have not developed your consciousness, then you become a remote-viewing technician, rather than a spiritual master. Be a master first. Master your consciousness and know God. Then you can play safely in the psychic playground. Turn your head in the right direction first—facing the divine realm. Then you will never go astray.

Now is the time to overcome psychic deception, eliminate spiritual gullibility, and embrace spiritual discernment. You are an all-powerful being. Only you must clear the channels for God to express through. By getting out of your own way, you can have the experiences you seek—experiences of the true realm of Spirit. Trust in God to be your only guru, and all will be well.

In the next chapter, you will learn how to heal the mental, astral, and environmental realms, so that you can contact the spiritual realm and receive your messages clearly.

Chapter 7
CLEARING the PATHWAY to GOD

"Once you replace negative thoughts with positive ones,
you'll start having positive results."
—Willie Nelson

To maintain your mind on a high vibrational level, apposite for hearing the voice of God, it is essential to learn spiritual mind healing. With the methods in this chapter, you will heal the astral/mental plane and thereby realize the spiritual level of consciousness required for this experience.

These healing methods are the keys to the kingdom of heaven. They will clear the way to effortlessly receiving clear, precise messages from God. Study this chapter carefully, for what you learn here is indispensable as you seek to hear the voice of God. This foundation will serve you for decades to come.

The Astral/Mental World

As you see in Figure 7a, the astral/mental world consists of the subconscious mind—both individual and collective. The false beliefs of this realm curb your ability to receive genuine experiences of God. Healing your subconscious mind rapidly moves you forward to inner divine contact.

The Astral/Mental World

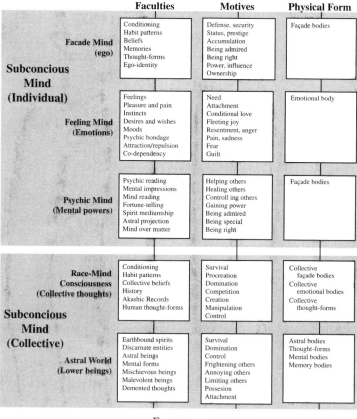

		Faculties	Motives	Physical Form
Subconcious Mind (Individual)	**Facade Mind (ego)**	Conditioning Habit patterns Beliefs Memories Thought-forms Ego-identity	Defense, security Status, prestige Accumulation Being admired Being right Power, influence Ownership	Façade bodies
	Feeling Mind (Emotions)	Feelings Pleasure and pain Instincts Desires and wishes Moods Psychic bondage Attraction/repulsion Co-dependency	Need Attachment Conditional love Fleeting joy Resentment, anger Pain, sadness Fear Guilt	Emotional body
	Psychic Mind (Mental powers)	Psychic reading Mental impressions Mind reading Fortune-telling Spirit mediumship Astral projection Mind over matter	Helping others Healing others Controll ing others Gaining power Being admired Being special Being right	Façade bodies

Subconcious Mind (Collective)	**Race-Mind Consciousness (Collective thoughts)**	Conditioning
		Habit patterns
		Collective beliefs
		History
		Akashic Records
		Human thought-forms
			Survival
			Procreation
			Domination
			Competition
			Creation
			Manipulation
			Control
				Collective
				  façade bodies
				Collective
				  emotional bodies
				Collective
				  thought-forms

	Astral World (Lower beings)	Earthbound spirits Discarnate entities Astral beings Mental forms Mischievous beings Malevolent beings Demented thoughts	Survival Domination Control Frightening others Annoying others Limiting others Possesion Attachment	Astral bodies Thought-forms Mental bodies Memory bodies

Figure 7a

The false beliefs of the astral/mental world muddy your mind with preconceived notions, thought patterns, and erroneous constructs that form a dense filter of negative energies. How can you heal this block? By using a few simple affirmative prayers at the appropriate time in specific situations. In this chapter, you will learn how and when to use these.

THE POWER OF THOUGHT

A wise man once said: *"All that we are is the result of what we have thought.... If a man speaks or acts with an evil thought, pain follows him, as the wheel follows the foot of the ox that draws the carriage.... If a man speaks or acts with a pure thought, happiness follows him, like a shadow that never leaves him."*

This is the first verse, therefore presumably the most important verse, of Lord Buddha's foremost scripture, the *Dhammapada*. Buddha states here that thought, speech, and action are the primary causes and determining factors of your life.

Many great thinkers agree:

"If you believe you can do a thing, or if you believe
that you cannot, you are right."
—Henry Ford

"You become what you most think about."
—Earl Conant

"A sincere belief that anything is so will make it so."
—William Blake

"Human beings, by changing the inner attitudes of their minds, can
change the outer aspects of their lives."
—William James

"The mind is its own place and in itself, can make
a Heaven of Hell, a Hell of Heaven."
—John Milton

The Upanishads of India say: *"A person consists of desires. And as is his desire, so is his will; and as is his will, so is his deed; and whatever deed he does, that he will reap."*[1] The Bible concurs: *"For as he thinketh in his heart, so is he."*[2] *"It is done unto you according to your belief."*[3]

The basic message of all these ancient and modern quotations is that you are the sole author of your destiny. You create your own future through:

- Thoughts (Beliefs)
- Words (Speech)
- Deeds (Action)

For detailed information about how you create your destiny, please read and study the first six chapters of my book *Miracle Prayer*.

How can you use this powerful knowledge of self-empowerment to improve conditions in your life? How can you eliminate false concepts and thereby open your mind to the message of God? Remember that the entire teaching of Divine Revelation is based on one principle: *"Ask, and it shall be given you."*[4]

By asking, you can receive divine guidance, and, by asking, you can transform your mind. You can use the healing affirmations in this chapter to change your mind from muddiness to pristine clarity—just by asking.

Methods of Spiritual Healing

Now you will learn these proven methods of spiritual healing that can transform your mind, body, and emotions:

- **Self-Authority Affirmation**: Become more powerful, centered, and balanced, and prevent "psychic sponge syndrome."
- **Prayer for Protection**: Develop spiritual self-defense and experience the divine presence.
- **Pillar of Light Visualization**: Fill your energy field with divine protection.
- **Divine Light Prayer**: Heal, clear, lift, and energize your energy field.
- **Thought-Form Healing**: Transform negative thoughts and emotions.
- **Astral-Entity Healing Affirmation**: Heal dense vibrations in the atmosphere.
- **Psychic-Tie–Cut Healing Affirmation**: Release undue attachments and addictions.
- **Façade-Body Healing Affirmation**: Let go of old habits and conditioning.

You can transform your mind and rejuvenate your body with these powerful techniques, which can heal yourself and others. Use them during meditation and everyday life, and any time you are attempting to hear the voice of God.

IMPORTANT: When praying for another person, rather than saying "I," "me," or "myself," in the affirmation, simply substitute the name of the person for whom you are praying.

SELF-AUTHORITY AFFIRMATION

The Self-Authority Affirmation helps you develop and maintain a powerful sense of self-reliance and inner strength. With this affirmation, you can overcome what I call "psychic sponge syndrome." A psychic sponge unconsciously absorbs atmospheric influences indiscriminately, as a sponge absorbs water. When you invite mental/astral rubbish into your energy field, your mind becomes a muddy receptacle—incapable of receiving clear divine guidance. Therefore, it is vital to say the following affirmation aloud, preferably in a strong voice, before attempting to hear the voice of God:

I AM in control. I AM one with God.

I AM the only authority in my life.

I AM divinely protected by the light of my being.

I close off my aura and body of light

To all but my own God self.

Thank you, God, and SO IT IS.

Please speak this affirmation three times now in a strong, clear voice. Then notice how you feel. Do you sense greater strength, power, and centeredness? Do you feel more inner stability and balance? This affirmation will help you connect with God and your own higher self.

Use the Self-Authority Affirmation:

- Before meditation and before sleep.
- During meditation when you feel out of control.
- To prepare to hear the voice of God.
- Whenever you feel apprehensive, afraid, or out of sorts.
- Before and after meeting any client or business associate.
- Repeat several times before any intimidating situation, such as a test, interview, audition, or meeting.
- To pray for another person's self-authority and self-reliance.

Divine Revelation student Michelle Chua, an operations manager from Portland, says: *"I know that I am in control right now instead of allowing others' advice to control and influence my state of being. I know that God is within me and protects me. There is no place for fear to reside. All is well."*

PRAYER FOR PROTECTION

The Prayer for Protection helps you maintain spiritual self-defense, divine protection, and intimacy with God. It allows you to feel God's presence and brings comfort, solace, and inspiration.

This prayer is used every Sunday throughout the world in New Thought churches, such as Church of Religious Science, Science of Mind, and Unity Church. James Dillet Freeman, Unity Church's poet laureate, composed the first four lines and last line of this prayer in 1941, during World War II, to give comfort to soldiers in the trenches:

> The light of God surrounds me;
> The love of God enfolds me;
> The power of God protects me;
> The presence of God watches over me;
> The mind of God guides me;
> The life of God flows through me;
> The laws of God direct me;
> The wisdom of God abides within me;
> The joy of God uplifts me;
> The strength of God renews me;
> The beauty of God inspires me;
> Wherever I AM, God is! And all is well!
> —James Dillet Freeman
> (Reprinted with permission from Unity, *www.unityonline.org.*)

This Prayer for Protection is so well known that, in July 1969, on *Apollo 11*, the first manned flight to land on the moon, astronaut and Lunar Module pilot Colonel Edwin Eugene "Buzz" Aldrin, Jr., carried it with him on his historic moonwalk.

Use the Prayer for Protection:

- Before you go into meditation.
- As you prepare to receive messages from God.
- Whenever you feel the feel lonely, afraid, or in need of divine protection.

- Whenever you want to experience God's presence.
- To pray for protection for another person.

PILLAR OF LIGHT VISUALIZATION

The Pillar of Light Visualization is an intentional meditation that fills your entire energy field with a shield of divine light, healing, and protection. Here is how it is done:

Visualize a beautiful, dazzling sun or brilliant divine globe of immeasurable light and glory above your head. This sphere of light might be white, gold, or another beautiful color that comes to mind. Think of this sun as the light of God.

Next, imagine a shining ray streaming down from this sun through the center midline of your body, from the top of your head down to your toes. This magnificent ray begins to glow and illumine your body from within. Streams from this ray start to radiate from the energy-center hubs (chakras) in your subtle body. These radiations become more luminous and intense. As they extend outward, they fill your energy field, forming a beauteous pillar of light.

This light pillar radiates and vibrates within and around you. It pervades your body and extends beyond your body as a column of divine protection, light, love, and energy. As you continue to imagine this pillar of God's armor of security, say the Prayer for Protection (on page 100) aloud, in a clear, strong voice.

To learn more about your subtle body and energy centers, otherwise known as chakras, please read my books *Exploring Auras* and *Exploring Chakras*.

Use the Pillar of Light Visualization:

- Before you leave your home.
- Before you enter a place or situation where you need protection.
- Before any intimidating situation or meeting.
- Whenever you want to experience divine comfort and security.
- As you prepare to receive clear messages from God.

DIVINE LIGHT PRAYER

The Divine Light Prayer increases God's light in your mind, body, and surroundings. It lifts your vibration and transmutes negative thoughts, emotions, and other discordant energies. It clarifies, invigorates, and energizes your energy field, and prevents psychic attack, psychic vampirism, and psychic sponge syndrome. To learn more, please read my book *Exploring Auras.*

Let there be light.
The holy light of God fills and encompasses me now.
With light of immeasurable beauty and glory.
Jesus Christ now fills and surrounds me
With a radiant golden sphere of protective light.
Archangel Michael now stands sentry
Above, below, and on every side of this sphere,
Waving his blue flame sword of truth and protection.
The mystic white fire of the Holy Spirit
Lifts my vibration now and brings perfect peace.
The violet, cleansing flame of Saint Germaine
Swirls through me now, purifying my energy field.
Mother Mary's pink light of unconditional love
Now touches me with gentleness.
Mahavatar Babaji's clear light of enlightenment
Now illumines my mind and purifies my soul.
I AM now lovingly lifted, healed, and cleansed
By the pure light of God's love,
Under grace, in God's own wise and perfect ways.
Thank you, God, and SO IT IS.

Use the Divine Light Prayer:

- To prepare to meditate or to receive clear messages from God.
- Whenever you want to connect with God.
- When you want divine protection, light, and energy.
- To prepare a room and/or a group for meditation.
- To pray for another person to receive divine light.

THOUGHT-FORM HEALING AFFIRMATION

Thought-forms are beliefs, habits, and patterns so persistent that they crystallize into subtle form. If you are attempting to hear the voice of God without success, then erroneous thought-forms are probably blocking the way. If your mind is stuck on the surface level, and deep meditation is difficult, then negative thought-forms are likely preventing you from going deep.

The Thought-Form Healing Affirmation is your most useful ally in your process of receiving messages from the voice of God. Whenever you feel stuck, confused, or simply clueless about what to do, this affirmation will help clear the way.

This affirmation has two blank spaces. As you read it, when you come to the first blank space, close your eyes and say whatever negative thoughts and emotions come up for you. Then fill the second blank space with positive statements that reverse the negative feelings you previously mentioned. In other words, if you said "sadness, depression, self-hatred, and unworthiness," now you would say "happiness, energy, self-love, and self-worth."

Use this simple affirmation anytime to release negative thoughts and emotions, and replace them with positive ones:

I now invoke the Holy Spirit
To heal, release, lift, and let go
Of all thoughts and emotions
That no longer serve me.
I release from my mind all thoughts of
(<u>negative thoughts</u>).
These thoughts are lifted
Into the light of God's love and truth.
I now welcome positive, supportive
Life-enhancing thoughts of
(<u>positive thoughts</u>).
I AM in control of my mind.
I AM the only authority in my life.
Thank you, God, and SO IT IS.

Use the Thought-Form Healing Affirmation:
- Before going into meditation.
- During meditation, if your mind is stuck in surface chatter.

- During meditation, when embroiled in negative thoughts and emotions.
- To prepare your mind to receive divine messages.
- If you are in a bad mood and want to feel uplifted.
- Whenever you need physical, mental, emotional, or spiritual healing.
- Whenever you want to heal the mind, body, or emotions of another person.

Kate O'Hara, a producer from Chicago, describes: *"Divine Revelation is helping me to look at fear, and to learn to protect myself from it. Also, that there can be no fear when love is present."*

A chiropractor from Denver, Sarah Worthley, writes: *"I cleared the negative energy that says I can't be clear about divine revelation. I faced fears of owning this power."*

For more information about the mental body and how to use the Thought-Form Healing Affirmation, please study my books *Divine Revelation, Exploring Meditation,* and *Exploring Auras.*

Astral-Entity Healing Affirmation

Astral entities are heavy, dense energy bodies. These vibrational black holes are discarnate beings or confused spirits in the astral realm. We discussed astral entities at length in Chapter 6. Such beings are the converse of anything divine, inspiring, or wise. Inflating their ego by respecting them as a source of wisdom does not serve them. Receiving messages from them does not serve you.

Astral entities do not necessarily have malevolent intentions. But they can give you messages, influence your mind, or take over your body. They can interfere with your ability to hear God's voice. In fact, they might masquerade as divine beings. However, most of them are lost and confused, and simply need a little encouragement to move into the divine light.

Whenever you sense the presence of astral entities, speak this healing affirmation immediately. It is addressed directly to the entities needing healing. Speak lovingly, clearly, and firmly to the entities and guide them into God's light, where they belong.

Dear ones,
You are unified in love with the truth of your being.
You are one with God and with your own higher self.

God's love and God's light fill and surround you now.
You are free from all negative vibrations and emotions.
You are free to move into the divine light now.
I call forth the Holy Spirit and the angelic beings of light,
To lead you by the hand
To your perfect place of divine expression.
You are blessed, forgiven, and released,
Into the love, light, and wholeness
Of your own higher self.
Go now in peace and love.

Use the Astral-Entity Healing Affirmation:

- During meditation whenever an entity interferes.
- If an astral entity tries to give you a message or interrupt a divine message.
- Whenever you feel a dense, creepy, heavy vibration or energy drain.
- When you wake up with a nightmare.
- When a child has a nightmare, a tantrum, or emotional outburst.
- When you feel adversely influenced or out of control.
- If you feel psychosomatic headaches or other pains.
- When someone is oppressed or possessed by an entity and needs healing.
- To pray for a person who is mentally ill.
- To clear a haunted house or building.

Albert Marsh, a retired architect from Los Angeles, describes: "*About 15 years ago I was in love with a man who was very difficult to get along with, probably because of entity influence, but this was before I knew about such things. He died, and, although I had already split up with him, I really loved him. I grieved deeply for him for well over a year. Something would remind me of our love and I would burst into hysterical tears. I happened to mention this to Ann Meyer, who originated our teaching along with her husband, Peter. She immediately recognized that my ex was still around me and causing me grief. She said the simple Astral Entity Healing Prayer, and after a last outburst of tears, he apparently was sent into the light. I was never bothered again, and I was so impressed that I took the beginner's course in our teaching, and now I am teaching Divine Revelation many years later.*"

Psychic-Tie–Cut Healing Affirmation

A psychic tie is an undue attachment, repulsion, or resistance to any person, place, thing, organization, situation, circumstance, memory, experience, or addiction that influences you adversely. Psychic ties are made of negative emotions and memories left over from detrimental encounters and experiences.

For example, after you argue with your boss, what remains? An energetic cord, rope, or string, composed of thought-forms, that connects your energy field with that of your boss. Thus, you have psychic ties with loved ones, co-workers, and others.

Psychic ties are in the astral/mental realm, and can be seen or felt with subtle senses. They often manifest behaviorally as obsessions, co-dependent relationships, compulsive thoughts, habitual behaviors, workaholism, or addictions.

Many people exclaim, "Oh, I have a psychic tie with him; we have a karmic connection!" as though this were a great blessing. Psychic ties are no blessing. Always harmful and never useful, they cause tension, frustration, addiction, and slavery. It is imperative to always cut and release them.

Psychic ties are not love ties. True love bonds are unbreakable golden ties of harmony and unconditional love that connect people on the spiritual plane. Such bonds are sacred and can never be cut. Love ties bring people together, but psychic ties drive them apart.

Many people are afraid to cut psychic ties. They believe that, by cutting them, they will be isolated from loved ones. But here is the truth: I guarantee that, if you cut psychic ties daily with your spouse, family members, and co-workers, you will have closer, more intimate relationships. You will not lose your loved ones. You will find yourself. Your relationships will improve immediately and continue to improve as you cut psychic ties every day. Use this affirmation to cut psychic ties:

> I call upon the Holy Spirit to now lovingly
> Cut any and all psychic ties between
> (myself—or name of person praying for)
> and (name of person, place, or thing cutting ties with).
> These psychic ties are now lovingly and completely
> Cut, cut, cut, cut, cut, cut, cut, cut, healed, blessed,
> Loved, dissolved, released, lifted, and let go

Into the light of God's love and truth.
Thank you, God, and SO IT IS.

In addition to this prayer, you can visualize a sword, knife, or scissors cutting the ties. You might pretend to hold the cutting instrument in your hand, and, as you speak the prayer, cut the ties with your hand or a sweeping gesture of your arm.

Use the Psychic-Tie–Cut Healing Affirmation:

- If you cannot go deep in meditation or cannot hear the voice of God due to a distraction or mental fixation on a person or thing.
- Whenever you feel pulled or tugged by someone or something.
- If you feel angry or resentful, or feel wronged or harmed by someone or something.
- When you are overly attached, dependent, or addicted to someone or something.
- When you feel dominated or controlled by someone or something.
- To pray for another person to cut psychic ties with someone or something influencing them adversely.

Evelyn Tan from Singapore, a travel agent, describes: *"I'm very glad to learn your methods of healing, especially the cutting of psychic ties. I believe they help to remove any obstacles and put me in the right connection to God."*

Travis Wyly, a chiropractor from England, Arkansas, reports: *"I have found the healing prayers for cutting psychic ties to be especially useful. I found that I have psychic ties not only to people, but to expectations, desires, beliefs, and attitudes, and, as I've cut those ties, my energy has been free to do other things."*

FAÇADE-BODY HEALING AFFIRMATION

Façade bodies are energetic armors made of thoughts, emotions, patterns, or habits condensed into densely packed, crystallized mental form. These subtle bodies mask and conceal your true self. You could be wearing several façade bodies at any given time. Each façade body is composed of thought-forms related to a particular strongly held belief.

For instance, you might wear a façade body of poverty, fear, self-doubt, or unworthiness. Maybe you are clad in an erroneous archetype, such as the "loner," "critic," "perfectionist," "rebel," "martyr," "conman," "sycophant," or "trickster." Certainly you can identify various façades in your own psyche.

Let us now heal a façade body that has been troubling you. Create a title or phrase that describes it. In the following affirmation you will state the name of the façade body in the blank space.

I call upon the Holy Spirit to now lovingly
Heal and release any and all façade bodies
That have prevented me from
Expressing my true nature of being.
All façade bodies of (name of façade body)
Are now lovingly cracked open, crumbled up,
Dissolved, healed, released, blessed, let go,
And lifted into the light of God's love and truth.
Thank you, God, and SO IT IS.

Use the Façade Body Healing Affirmation:
- When you cannot go deep in meditation due to a dense thought-form.
- To release a thought pattern that prevents you from hearing the voice of God.
- Whenever you want to heal a strong belief or emotion.
- When you want to make a life change.
- To pray for others who want to transform conditions in their life.

HEALING SIGNALS

How would you decide which healing affirmation to use in a given situation? The answer is what I call "healing signals." Healing signals are signs that particular energetic problems are present and therefore necessitate specific healing affirmations. The most common problems are (1) thought-forms—negative thoughts and emotions; (2) attachments, repulsions, and resistances—psychic ties; (3) astral influences; and (4) densely packed crystallized beliefs—façade bodies.

Therefore, if you need to use the Thought-Form Healing Affirmation in a particular situation, you will receive a "thought-form healing signal." If the Astral-Entity Healing Affirmation is required, you will receive an "astral entity healing signal." In other words, each healing signal corresponds with a healing prayer.

At any moment, your mind can be a garden of delight, a hellish nightmare, or something in between, depending on your unconscious choice.

When your mind needs attention, your wonderful internal checks-and-balance system gives you a signal to warn you.

Healing signals are often uncomfortable or distasteful sensory experiences. That is because God is sounding an alarm to get your attention. These signals act like the body's need to experience pain. Pain is your friend. It indicates that something is amiss. Without pain, you would never recognize that you are ill. Similarly, healing signals often involve discomfort.

Healing signals are diagnostic tools. The signal identifies the problem, but does not show who needs to be healed. However, if you are thinking or speaking about a person as you get a healing signal, then likely that person needs healing. So stop for a moment and speak or whisper the appropriate healing prayer.

When you receive a healing signal, you might mistake it for a physical disease. Many of my students discovered that various chronic pains were actually healing signals. Linda Vernon, a trucker from Brandon, Florida, writes: *"Susan did a healing prayer for me to release psychic ties that had literally been pushing me down as a weighted yoke across my upper back. After her healing, I was able to sit up straight without pain, which hadn't happened in a very long time. The heaviness was completely gone."*

Healing signals are unique and personal. For instance, your healing signal for astral entities will probably differ from mine; however, your personal healing signals always remain the same. So, for example, your healing signal for astral entities will stay the same throughout your life.

The easiest way to identify your healing signals is to pay attention to uncomfortable sensations and situations. For example, if you enter a hospital, mental institution, or prison, you might feel a drain of energy along with a unique discomfort in your body. When you get that feeling, begin to say the healing prayers in this chapter. Whatever healing prayer eliminates your pain is the appropriate healing prayer corresponding with that healing signal.

Curt De Groat, a psychic from New York, describes his healing signal: *"I had been a channel for 10 years before meeting Susan Shumsky, and [had] meditated for 15 years. I directed a Sanctuary of the Ascended Masters. I had to close it down because of illness. I was constantly feeling drained and like I was being punched in the navel. When Susan gave me the breakthrough, she had to do many healings and clearings for me. I discovered that the feeling of being punched in the navel was a signal that I needed to use the Astral Healing Prayer. Eventually the signal lessened for me so that now when it does happen it is no longer an incapacitating experience."*

You might get more than one healing signal at once. In such cases, it is wise to say whatever healing prayers are needed. You have possibly been receiving healing signals your entire life. By using the healing affirmations

regularly, you will begin to identify healing signals as symptoms corresponding with the affirmations.

Here are a few sample healing signals identified by my students. Please
remember that you will only receive one signal for each healing affirmation, and
it will never change. Your signals will likely differ from those described here.

- **Sample Astral-Entity Healing Signals**: vision of demon or
  gray entity, black dot or black aura, or thick black lines;
  feeling of nausea, body pain, or tight muscle; hearing
  moaning, negative voices, hellish groans or screams, maniacal
  laughing, or other creepy sounds; feeling creepy sensations;
  smelling sickening odor; nasty taste in mouth or dry mouth.

- **Sample Thought-Form Healing Signals**: vision of a gray
  cloud, brick wall, spaghetti or fire in the brain; feeling
  depressed, pressure in chest, weight on shoulders, weight on
  body, carrying a burden, headache, muscle twitch, muscle
  tightening, pain in eyes; smelling noxious odor; hearing the
  sound of thunder or sirens blaring.

- **Sample Psychic-Tie–Healing Signals**: vision of strings or
  cords, fishing net, trap, grid, thick ropes, umbilical cord;
  obsessive fixations; feeling of tugging, tied up with rope,
  pulled in stomach, body pain, muscle tightening, choking,
  imprisonment, entrapment, suffocating, hooks in back.

- **Sample Façade-Body Healing Signals**: vision of a mask or
  straightjacket; feeling of plate armor, claustrophobia, band
  around head, trapped in cage, box, or elevator, locked in jail.

Often people get healing signals and then unconsciously describe them,
such as: "I'm up against a brick wall," "So attached to him," "At the end of my
rope," "Feel smothered," "Seeing red," "Sick to my stomach," "Hear sirens,"
"Feel weighed down," "Breaking my back," "Joined at the hip," "Boxed in,"
"Between a rock and a hard place," "Chasing my own tail," "On fire," "About
to explode," "Weighing on my mind," "The last straw," "Give me some breathing space," "Dog is at the door," "Feel so small," "I'm suffocating," "Holding on
for dear life," "Brain is scrambled," "He really turns me off," "I could scream,"
"Ton of bricks on my shoulders," "I'm drowning," "Green with envy," "Driving
me up a wall," "I'm turning red," and so forth.

It may take time for you to identify your healing signals. Therefore, if
possible, I recommend you receive your healing signals on one of our retreats
or from a qualified Divine Revelation teacher. You will find information about

these opportunities and a list of teachers on our Website at *www.divinerevelation.org*. Once you recognize your signals, use the chart in Figure 7b to record them.

Healing Signals

Thought-Form Healing Signal	
Psychic-Tie-Cut Healing Signal	
Astral-Entity Healing Signal	
Façade-Body Healing Signal	

Figure 7b

In addition to learning the healing affirmations in this chapter, please study my book *Exploring Auras*, which teaches dozens of powerful healing prayers, and *Divine Revelation*, which explains the healing prayers in greater detail.

YOUR HOMEWORK ASSIGNMENT

In order to maintain mental and environ-mental clarity, it is vital to use the healing affirmations regularly. Therefore, your homework assignment is to check in with how you are feeling at least three times a day, and then say whichever healing affirmation in this chapter is needed at the time. If you notice negative experiences more often, then use the appropriate affirmations whenever they are needed. Do this for the next 30 days. Then send an e-mail to divinerev@aol.com, or write a letter to Susan Shumsky, Divine Revelation, P.O. Box 7185, New York, NY 10116. Write at least two paragraphs describing the amazing experiences you are having in your life and in the lives of others as a result of using these healing affirmations.

Now that you have learned basic healing prayers to help you hear the voice of God clearly, in the next chapter, you will use these prayers in conjunction with my 10-test system for verifying the authenticity of inner messages.

chapter 8

10 TESTS of SPIRITUAL DISCERNMENT

"Don't think you're on the right road just because it's a well-beaten path."
—Anonymous

In the next two chapters, you will learn how to test the divine messages that you receive with a 10-test system. Every time I receive an inner message, I use these 10 tests to determine whether the message is from God, from my mind or ego, wishful thinking, an entity, or environ-mental static. These 10 tests are essential for anyone who desires to hear the voice of God clearly.

When you use this system, all 10 tests must pass the evaluation. Not one test, two tests, or five tests. All 10. Therefore, as you move down the list, validating your message, make a mental checklist. Every test will either pass or fail. All 10 tests must pass in order for you to be reasonably sure that the message is from God.

Now, let us learn the tests.

TEST 1: EXPERIENCE OF GOD

10 Ways to Test Your Message

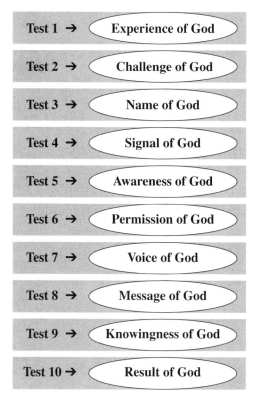

Figure 8a

How would you feel if God spoke to you? You would feel loved, healed, and inspired. You would experience joy and fulfillment. Do you believe in a God of retribution? Or do you believe God is pure love? If you are really in communication with God, you would be uplifted—not judged, condemned, and sent to hell.

When you are in touch with God, you experience:

- Unconditional Love
- Safety, Security, Protection
- Happiness, Joy, Light
- Peace, Tranquility, Serenity
- Contentment
- Perfection
- Oneness, Wholeness, Unity

The most important of the 10 Tests of Spiritual Discernment is the Experience Test. And the most important feelings are wholeness, oneness, and unity. That is because wholeness cannot be fabricated by astral entities, because they are not in that elevated state. They are scattered, confused, and incoherent. Therefore, under entity influence, you will feel disintegration—not integration.

Also, contacting the mental world cannot make you feel whole. This is the realm of duality, not unity. Oneness is felt solely in the presence of God. Thus, if you are unhappy, agitated, fragmented, or other negative emotions, then the test has failed.

When Test 1 Fails

If you are experiencing the spiritual feelings described when you are in touch with God, then the Experience Test has passed. If you are not, then the test has failed, and it is time to return to oneness, unity, and contentment. How would you do that?

Let us perform an experiment. With eyes open, please notice how you are feeling in body, mind, and spirit. Now close your eyes and take three deep breaths. Observe how you feel after taking the breaths. Are you more relaxed, connected, and at peace? This demonstrates firsthand how breathing can immediately bring you closer to God. Here are some ways to help you return to a state of oneness:

- **Breathe:** Often you are not connected with God because you are not deep enough in meditation. Take deep breaths and relax your body and mind. Get centered, balanced, and focused. Or practice *pranayama* or other breathing exercises. (To learn pranayama, refer to my books *Exploring Meditation*, *Exploring Chakras*, or *Exploring Auras*.)

- **Ask to Go Deeper:** Call upon God or a divine being by name, and ask to be taken deeper. For example, you might say, "Jesus, please come now and take me deeper," or "God, please take me deeper," or "Lord Buddha, please take me deeper."

- **Heal:** Use the Thought-Form Healing Affirmation on page 103, or another appropriate healing affirmation from Chapter 7.

- **Pray:** Say a prayer. Craft your own prayer, or read a favorite prayer from the Bible, prayer book, scripture of your choice, or my book *Miracle Prayer*.

- **Meditate:** Go into deep meditation, experience the stillness, and reconnect with God.

- **Connect:** Go outside and take a walk in nature. Feel the presence of God in all life.

- **Relax:** Lie down on your back. Relax and feel the energy in your body until you sense a feeling of unity with God.

- **Exercise:** Practice yoga asanas, Tai Chi, Brain Gym, or other spiritual practices to become centered, balanced, and energized.

These are just a few of the many ways you can reconnect with Spirit.

Beverly Marrick, a writer from Salt Lake City, described that during her Divine Revelation Breakthrough, she *"felt a clearing of the mind for the first time, which allowed me to also meditate for the first time. I came with expectations of positive visual experiences as opposed to the negative I typically receive, and was surprised to have no visuals aside from the bright light."*

A receptionist from St. Louis reported: *"It really took me a long time to calm down because thoughts were racing. I was frustrated and blocked. I had trouble meditating and relaxing. After I took a lot of deep breaths I began to go deeper, get calm, and release my baggage. Then I finally got my clear signal and message from the Holy Spirit."*

An Exception to the Rule

There is one exception to the Experience Test—a situation in which an individual might be fully connected with God, yet not peaceful or relaxed. For people in mortal danger, the sympathetic nervous system produces the fight-or-flight response. Although there is no love, light, or joy, such people might be in full contact with Spirit. Time seems to slow down or stand still. Primal instinct takes over, and a sense of alertness, assuredness, and calm emerges. In that life-threatening situation, they know exactly what to do, with complete confidence.

For example, Tova Prager of San Diego, California, describes: *"A friend was teaching me to drive. I didn't know much about cars, but she thought I knew more. So I was behind the wheel for the first time. A slow-moving lettuce truck was in front of us. She said, 'Just speed up. We're going to pass him.' I said, 'Okay.' I sped up, but then got scared and jammed [on] the brakes. Bam. We hit the truck and spun around and around. Suddenly, lettuce was everywhere. My six-month-old daughter was in the car, seated between us. A few minutes before, she had been seated on my friend's lap. But the most amazing thing was, while everything was spinning, the three of us were perfectly calm and did not feel we needed to hold onto anything. It was like an angel had come into the car and held us solidly in place like we were sitting at home on a sofa—not in motion. When the car finally stopped, the truck driver (thank God nothing happened to him) came over. He got down on his knees and said, 'Santa Maria, oh my God.' He thought we were dead. The car was totaled and completely demolished. Four tires were blow out. But we walked out like nothing happened."*

After Test 1 has made a passing grade on your checklist, then you can move on to Test 2. Make sure that, as you move through the tests, each test is passed before going to the next one.

TEST 2: CHALLENGE OF GOD

If a stranger were to knock on your door, would you invite him to come in and take over your home? No. Before opening your door, you would ask who sent the stranger. Similarly, before letting anyone or anything give you a message, first make sure it comes from the spiritual plane. Challenge that being by asking one of the following questions:

- "Do you come in the name of God?"
- "Do you come in the name of the Christ?"
- "Do you come as the Christ?"

Whenever you contact any being, first ask one of these questions. You will receive a "yes," a "no," or no answer at all. Please do not get "creative" with this test. Just use the question exactly as worded.

Some people believe that a faker spirit will answer this question with a lie. After teaching tens of thousands of people, I can say with assurance that if you ask one of these exact questions, you will not have this problem. Often, a faker spirit will not say no. It simply will not answer. However, if there is no answer, then consider that the same as a "no."

Many spiritual teachers advise their students to ask, "Do you come in the light?" However, I do not recommend this. What light are you speaking of? The 10-watt lightbulb? The fluorescent light? The light of burning hell? Bud Light? Miller Light?

Let us now discuss how you would get a "yes" or "no" response in the answer to your Challenge question. Here are several ways:

- **Clairaudience:** You might hear "yes" or "no" in your inner ear.
- **Clairvoyance:** You might see the word "yes" or the word "no" in your inner vision. Or you might see a green light for "yes" and a red light for "no." Or another visual symbol that represents "yes" and one that represents "no."
- **Clairsentience:** You might sense a specific body feeling representing "yes" and another representing "no."
- **Body Movements:** You might get a finger tapping, hand movement, head movement, or other body movement for "yes" and another for "no."
- **Muscle-Testing:** Use muscle-testing to get "yes" and "no" responses. A simple method is taught in *Exploring Auras*.
- **Intuitive Kinesiology:** Use dowsing instruments, such as a pendulum, L-rods, Y-rod, bobber, planchette, or table-tipping to get "yes" and "no" responses. (I teach many of these methods in *Exploring Auras* and *Divine Revelation*.)

Please now take a moment to ask God to indicate and verify your "yes" and "no" signals, through one of these methods. Please write your signals in Figure 8b, so you will remember them. If possible, contact a qualified Divine Revelation teacher to verify your signals. A list of those teachers is at *www.divinerevelation.org*.

Verifying "Yes" and "No" Signals

1. "YES" SIGNAL	
2. "NO" SIGNAL	

Figure 8b

When Test 2 Fails

If you receive a "yes" response from your Challenge question, then the test has passed. However, if the answer to your Challenge question is a "no," or if you get no response, then take the following three steps:

1. **Heal All the Way**: My mentor Peter V. Meyer often said, "Heal first and ask questions later." In other words, without further inquiry, immediately use the Astral Entity Healing Affirmation on page 104. Heal the entity or faker spirit, and send it into the light. Then use the Self-Authority Affirmation on page 99.

2. **Breathe and Meditate**: Once you have healed the entity, take a few deep breaths. Then regroup and return to a deep meditative state.

3. **Ask Again**: After you have reconnected with Spirit, ask the Challenge question again until you receive a clear "yes."

If Test 2, the Challenge Test has passed, then move on to Test 3.

TEST 3: NAME OF GOD

When a stranger knocks at your door, would you open the door and say, "Come in"? Or would you first ask, "Who's there?" It is essential to first determine who or what is at your door. Get the calling card. Find out its name.

Every divine being has a name—even God has a name. The word G-O-D is a name. And there are many other divine names. Please refer to some of these names on page 35 of this book. Also, please review what we discussed about inner names on pages 46 to 48.

Perhaps when you ask for the name, you receive a name that makes you uncomfortable. Maybe it is an aspect of God that you do not believe in, or that is not part of your religion. Please remember that you have the right to refuse contact with any being, no matter what your reason. Therefore, only accept inner names that you feel comfortable with, and dismiss those that you do not want to work with.

> **BUYER BEWARE**: Be sure to check all 10 tests, not just Test 3. That is because faker spirits might give you a counterfeit name, often a biblical or "high"-sounding name, in order to impress you. Therefore, it is safer to work with names of God that you know and trust. However, do not be surprised if an unfamiliar, yet genuine, deity appears. Please consider that possibility. You might learn something new.

Do you know how to receive an inner name? Here are a few ways to discover the name of the being with whom you are in contact:

- **Hear the Name**: Receive the inner name through clairaudience. The name might occur to you in your inner ear, or you might hear an inner voice saying the name in your mind.

- **See the Name**: You might see the name with your inner eye. It may appear as letters, or you might see a figure that you recognize. For example, you might see Jesus Christ, Lord Krishna, Our Lady of Guadalupe, or another being in your inner vision. Even if you never hear the name, you will know the name by recognizing the figure.

- **Spell the Name**: You might use muscle-testing, dowsing, or intuitive kinesiology to spell out the name. Learn more about these methods in *Exploring Auras* and *Divine Revelation*.

When Test 3 Fails

If you have received a clear inner name, then the test has passed. What would you do if the inner name is not clear, or if you do not want to communicate with the being that comes to you? Here are some possibilities:

- **Heal All the Way**: Heal names you do not know and trust, whether or not you think they are astral entities. Use the Astral Entity Healing Affirmation on page 104. If it is a divine being, it will not be offended that you tried to heal it. If it is an entity, it will be healed and move into the light.

- **Use Trusted Names**: If you want to be absolutely safe, then only work with names that you know and trust.

- **Heal Your Mind:** If you are not getting the name clearly, then heal yourself. Use the Thought-Form Healing Affirmation on page 103. Or use other suitable healing prayers that are needed.

- **Go Deeper:** Take deep breaths and go deeper into meditation. Then ask for the name again until you receive it clearly.

- **Call on the Name:** At any time you can call upon any divine being or deity that you want to contact. For example, you might say, "Archangel Michael, please come to me now," "Jesus Christ, please come here now," "Kwan Yin, please come now," or "Hashem," please come now."

Test 4: Signal of God

The signal is the sign that you are in contact with a particular inner name. We discussed the signal on pages 48 to 51. I recommend that you reread and study that section thoroughly. To review briefly, your divine signals come in six possible ways:

- Seeing: Visual
- Hearing: Auditory
- Smelling: Olfactory
- Tasting: Gustatory
- Feeling: Kinesthetic
- Movement: Kinetic

The Signal is a crucial test, because it identifies the divine being that you are contacting. Getting its unique signal means that you are in contact with that particular divine being. You will receive that signal the entire time you are getting a clear message from that aspect of God. When the signal disappears, either you lost contact or the message is over. Pay attention to when the signal stops. That is the time for you to stop.

To illustrate this point, a channeler from California is known for speaking long discourses on philosophical topics. One evening I attended his presentation, which he channeled in a conscious state. He spoke through discourses from various beings, including Sananda and Saint Germaine. The following day, I approached him with some trepidation, because I did not want to offend him, and I explained that in the beginning of his speeches, I had experienced inner signals and divine feelings verifying his clarity, but, as he continued to speak, I lost my inner contact. He then openly admitted that he began each lecture with a clear inner contact, but when he realized he had lost his divine contact, he simply continued speaking, elaborating on the message. At that point he was no longer a divine messenger. He became a showman.

Signals are very useful, because they identify the specific aspect of God that you are communicating with. Your divine signals always stay the same. The signal may become subtler with time, but will always be the unique signal corresponding with that particular inner name.

Why is the signal so important? Because you can rely on this experience, which you probably have been receiving your entire life in every meditation. Divine signals elevate your spirit and attune you more powerfully to your higher self. Signals can be accurate gauges to measure the depth and clarity of your divine messages.

> **BUYER BEWARE:** Be certain to use all 10 tests along with the Signal Test. Astral entities might give you signals or try to imitate your divine signal. Psychic mediums have been receiving signals for centuries from astral beings, not divine beings. Always use the Challenge Test first before attempting to get your signal.

When Test 4 Fails

If you receive a clear, strong signal from the aspect of God whose name you have identified, then the Signal Test is passed. If you do not, the test has failed. What if the signal is missing, imprecise, or ambiguous?

- **Ask:** Call upon the name of the divine being from whom you want to get a signal. Then ask for your signal. You might say something like, "Mother Mary, please feed me your signal now," or "Lord Shiva, please give me your signal now." Remember, when you get a signal, ask for the name. When you get a name, ask for the signal. When you get the name and the signal, ask for the message. Always ASK.

- **Ask for Stronger Signal:** If the signal is not strong or clear, then call upon the divine being and ask the signal to be fed stronger. You might say, "Holy Spirit, please feed your signal stronger. Please make it stronger. Please feed your signal stronger," until you receive the signal clearly.

- **Heal All the Way:** Heal anything blocking the clear experience of your signal. Perhaps thought-forms, entities, psychic ties, or other negative energies stand in the way.

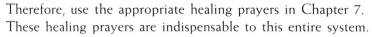

Therefore, use the appropriate healing prayers in Chapter 7. These healing prayers are indispensable to this entire system.

- **Breathe**: Take deep breaths and go deeper into meditation. Then ask the divine being to feed you the signal again.
- **Pray**: Speak prayers for clarity in receiving your inner signals. Use my book *Miracle Prayer* to help you compose prayers for clarity.

Test 5: Awareness of God

You can receive your divine messages with an alert, clear mind. There is no need to be unconscious in order to get messages from God; therefore, be awake and aware when receiving messages.

You may have seen channelers or psychic mediums who enter an unconscious trance-like stupor when receiving messages. After their reading or performance, they wake up and ask, "What did I say? I don't remember anything that happened." Then you are supposed to be impressed. You are expected to be in awe that this person checked out of the human hotel and let some strange, nameless entity check in and take over his body. This is not impressive. It is a dangerous game of psychic roulette.

Do you think God requires you to become unconscious in order to give you a message? Did God require Jesus, Moses, or other prophets to go unconscious? No. God's message is received in a conscious, alert state.

Although readings of unconscious mediums might be helpful for their clients, they are definitely not helpful for the mediums. Expert psychics, spiritual teachers, parapsychologists, psychologists, and researchers agree that the effect on those who engage in unconscious mediumship is as follows:

- Breaks the body/mind coordination.
- Causes illness.
- Causes early death.

I cannot overemphasize the dangers of practices that involve unconscious psychic mediumship or trance channeling. It is easy for a robber to plunder a vacant house with the owner elsewhere. In contrast, few thieves would risk entering a house when the owner is at home. Similarly, astral entities are more likely to enter your body when it is left untended and unoccupied. But when you are at home, centered, balanced, alert, awake, and grounded in your body, astral entities dare not enter.

There is only one safe way to receive inner messages in an unconscious state that is during sleep. You might receive divine revelations in your dreams.

However, if you get a nightmare, then I recommend using the Astral Entity Healing Affirmation on page 104 immediately. Also, say the Self-Authority Affirmation on page 99 to close off your aura every night, right before sleep.

When Test 5 Fails

If you are conscious and alert as you receive inner messages, then the test has passed. What would you do if you begin to go unconscious? How can you stay alert? Here are some guidelines:

- **Be Objective:** Do not be overly passive. Do not be too introverted or meditate too much. Lead a balanced life of meditation, prayer, healing, and dynamic activity.

- **Be Vigilant:** Do not open to unknown entities. Do not allow anything to "take over" you. Do not let yourself be used by anything or anyone. Do not make bargains or contracts with entities.

- **Wake Up:** If you find yourself going blank or unconscious during meditation, or if you notice something or someone trying to gain entry, then immediately open your eyes and say, in a loud voice, "I AM in control."

TEST 6: PERMISSION OF GOD

Now the first five tests have been passed. The next step is Test 6. You have a question in your mind that you want to ask God. Before asking your question, it is important to get permission from your higher self, from the person in question, or from God. Why? Because you might be asking an inappropriate question. So, use the three-part Permission Test.

1. **Can I?** The first part of Permission is "Can I get the answer?" This means, "Am I capable of receiving this message?" For example, imagine that you are a psychic and a client wants to ask questions about quantum physics. Yet you have no science background. The question then becomes: Even though you have never studied the subject of your client's inquiry, is your intuition good enough for you to receive clear answers?

2. **May I?** The second part of Permission is "May I ask this question?" This means, "Do I have consent to ask this?" Getting consent is important, especially when asking questions for or about other people.

For instance, you would probably not receive permission to satisfy your curiosity about how much money a friend makes. Another example would be asking God how to heal someone. You might not receive permission without that person's consent.

On the other hand, you might get permission to ask a question or do a healing, even without the person's consent, if it is for the best of all concerned. It is important in such cases to get permission from your higher self or from the higher self of that person. This is particularly important if the individual is unavailable to ask for permission.

3. **Is it highest wisdom?** This third part of the Permission Test means, "Is this the question that is best to ask?" There are three sections to "highest wisdom":

    A. **Is this for the good of all concerned?** This means, "Will receiving the answer to this question harm anyone, or will its effect be entirely beneficial?" Perhaps the answer to a particular question will cause negative repercussions.

    B. **Is this the best question to ask?** Perhaps you are wording the question incorrectly, or you are asking the wrong question. For instance, asking a confusing or vague question will result in an imprecise, unclear answer. Therefore, it is better to reword the question.

    C. **Am I ready to receive the answer?** Maybe you are unprepared to hear the answer or will not accept it.

When Test 6 Fails

If you receive a "yes" response when you ask your Permission question, then the test has passed. What would you do if you do not get permission? Take the three following steps:

1. **Discover Why**: Ask God to show you the reason you are not getting permission to ask your question.

2. **Make a Change**: Depending on the reason, you might change the question, reword it, or drop the question. Please study *Divine Revelation* for detailed information about how to word questions in order to receive clear answers.

3. **Make a Decision**: If you can change the question properly, then you might get permission. However, if you do not get permission, then do not proceed at this time. Ask again later.

TEST 7: VOICE OF GOD

Have you encountered mediums or trance channelers who speak in an accent different from their normal voice? Some of them conduct melodramatic performances, altering their voice, either consciously or unconsciously, to amaze, astonish, and create mystique. When they begin their reading or performance, suddenly they feign an Irish lilt, a bizarre brogue, or another strange, creepy accent.

Because the medium's voice changes as they purportedly channel the spirit, the client or audience is supposed to be impressed by such theatrics. Misguided, gullible followers are in awe, as though the weird accent adds value and glamour to the message.

A linguist named Sarah Thomason from the University of Pittsburgh conducted a scientific study on 11 channelers. She reported in *Psychology Today* that not one of those channelers spoke in an accent consistent with the time and place in which the entity supposedly lived. They were all fake![1]

Here are some reasons a channeler or medium might speak in a weird accent:

- **Faker Spirits:** The medium is channeling a faker spirit that is mimicking a bizarre accent in order to impress the client or audience.
- **Earthbound Spirit:** The medium is in contact with an entity from the lower astral realm that had a foreign accent when it was alive.
- **Performance:** The medium is staging a theatrical performance in order to impress the client or the audience.
- **Channeling the Departed:** There are very rare mediums that allow a spirit to use their body and vocal chords. These mediums sound exactly as that departed spirit did when alive.
- **Disbelief in Divine Contact:** Some psychics or mediums might receive authentic messages from the voice of God. But if they do not believe God can speak to them, then they will unconsciously sabotage those messages. Instead, they might invent an accent. This will give them "permission" to receive messages, because they unconsciously rationalize that, although it is not okay to receive messages from God, it is okay to get messages from entities. Such false beliefs invite lower vibrations, and soon astral entities take over.

Do you think God requires you to change your voice in order to give you a divine message? No. God's message comes in your own normal inner voice (your mind) and may be expressed in your own normal outer voice (your speech). The feeling of your voice might change when God speaks through you. It may become softer, sweeter, gentler, stronger, or more authoritative. But it will still sound like your own voice.

Beware of any voice that pounds in your head in an accusatory, overly aggressive tone. Here is an example:

Jamie Michaels, an art director from Detroit, wrote: *"I heard a voice tell me three separate times that I had to give up sex. The last time I heard the voice, it shouted in my ears so loud that I had to put my hands over my ears. It screamed, 'The wages of sin is death!' after I went ahead and had sex with my boyfriend about six weeks after the voice told me not to. Strange stuff to be hearing from someone that was not 'Christian' at that time."*

When Test 7 Fails

If the inner voice sounds normal, like your usual thoughts or usual voice, then the test has passed. If you hear an inner voice with a weird accent or harsh tone, what would you do? Here is the best way to handle the situation in three steps:

1. **Heal All the Way:** The moment that you hear or sense a strange voice, immediately use the Astral-Entity Healing Affirmation on page 104. Send the entity into the divine light.

2. **Breathe:** Then take a few deep breaths and go deeper into meditation.

3. **Start Again:** After going deep into meditation and getting connected with God, begin the process of using the 10 tests again. Go back to Test 1.

TEST 8: MESSAGE OF GOD

If you receive a message from the voice of God, what would the message be like? Would it be a message of judgment, anger, and vengeance? Or love, light, and peace? I believe that God is pure love; therefore, God's message can be described as:

- Loving
- No Judgment, No Guilt
- Healing
- Comforting

- Universal Truth
- Positive, Optimistic, and Helpful
- Inspiring and Uplifting
- Relevant, Practical, and Sensible
- Simplicity
- No Harm
- No Conditions or Demands
- No Threats or Fear
- No Control or Manipulation
- Freedom
- Ego Flattery
- No Irreversible Doom and Gloom
- Responsibility
- Unity
- Genuine Revelation

The Message Test is so complex that it cannot be adequately covered in this chapter. Therefore, Chapter 9 is devoted entirely to this test. Please study it carefully before attempting to use this 10-test system.

When Test 8 Fails

If the characteristics of the message are inspiring, positive, and so forth, as described, then the test has passed. But what if the message is judgmental, conditional, complicated, or otherwise unacceptable?

Please refer to Figure 8c on the following page. Perhaps the message was skewed by your subconscious mind's interference. Or an entity jumped in. Maybe it was distorted by your ego or false beliefs. Most likely, you were not deep enough in meditation, and you received your message from the surface level of mind. When you go deep into meditation, you will receive true spiritual messages. Here are ways to get a clear message:

- **Heal All the Way**: If you feel entity influence, then use the Astral-Entity Healing Affirmation on page 104. If your mind is in the way, use the Thought-Form Healing Affirmation on page 103. If you are influenced by a person or thing in your environment, use the Psychic-Tie–Cut Healing Affirmation on page 106.
- **Pray**: Read a prayer in a scripture of your choice, or a prayer from *Miracle Prayer*.

Receiving Clear Messages

Surface Mind or Environment	**Gross**	Mind receives messages from gross, surface level of mind or environment— or deep, subtle planes of Spirit.
Unconscious Mind or Ego		
Entities or Faker Spirits		Deeper Meditation = Clearer Messages.
TRUE VOICE OF GOD	**Subtle**	

Figure 8c

- **Breathe:** Take a few deep breaths and go into a deeper meditation.
- **Ask to Go Deeper:** Call upon an aspect of God and ask to be taken deeper. You might say, "Jesus, please take me into a deeper meditation," or "God, take me deeper."
- **Ask for Clarity:** Call upon an aspect of God and ask for clarity, or pray for clarity. You might say, "God, please clarify my mind and connect me with Spirit." Or you may compose a prayer by using the nine-step process taught in *Miracle Prayer*.

TEST 9: KNOWINGNESS OF GOD

When you receive a clear message from the voice of God, you know that you know, without knowing *how* you know. You just know it. You know beyond a shadow of doubt, with complete certainty and conviction.

Have you ever had the experience of "I just knew that I should have invested in that stock," "I knew I should have closed that business deal when I had a chance," or "I knew I should have avoided that relationship"? These are examples of inner knowingness.

Inner knowing is not the same as wishful or magical thinking. Wishful thinking is hoping that something is true, even though, in the back of your mind, your inner voice warns you that it is not. An example that some young women experience is: "Oh, I just know he's the right man for me." Her wishful thinking might say he is Mr. Right. But the "still small voice" of God, that tiny voice within her heart, may be screaming, "Run the other way as fast as you can!"

Other examples of wishful thinking might be: "Oh, I know I will become a famous actor within a year if I just move to Los Angeles," "Oh, I know I will win the lottery if I buy just one more ticket," "I know I can make him convert to my religion," or "I know I can make that woman love me." Listen to your inner voice, and do not accept the illusion of false hopes and magical thinking.

On the other hand, if the message is clear, then trust it. The true voice of God might give you guidance that appears unachievable, incredible, or impossible. Yet, if the message is true, then follow it, even if it seems difficult or challenging.

Inner knowingness means knowing with absolute conviction. If you know that the message from your inner voice is true, with complete certainty, beyond any doubt, then this test has passed.

When Test 9 Fails

What would you do if Test 9 has failed? What if your message does not sound right or feel right, or you mistrust the message? How would you get a clear message with the experience of inner knowingness? Here are some suggestions:

- **Heal All the Way:** The reason you are not getting inner knowingness is that your message is not clear. Use an appropriate healing prayer from Chapter 7 to heal whatever is preventing you from getting clear messages.

- **Pray:** Say a prayer that gives you greater confidence and inner assurance, such as a Psalm from the Bible, a prayer from your favorite scripture, or from *Miracle Prayer.*

- **Take a Few Deep Breaths:** One reason you are not getting clear messages is that you are not deep enough. By taking a few deep breaths, you can go deeper into the meditative state.

- **Ask to Go Deeper:** Call upon a divine being or your higher self to take you deeper. Simply say, "God, take me deeper," to enter a more profound meditative state.

- **Ask Question Again:** After you have healed your mind and achieved a deeper state of meditation, then ask your question again.

Test 10: Result of God

If you receive a true message from God, how would you feel? Would you be inspired and fulfilled? Or agitated and drained? If you were truly in touch with God, then you would be positively transformed and healed. You would feel:

-   **Relieved and Comforted**: God gives comfort and release from care.
-   **Healed, Vital, and Strong**: God brings restoration and wholeness.
-   **Confident, Empowered, and Assured**: God brings self-reliance, self-sufficiency, and certainty.
-   **Motivated, Inspired, and Elated**: God is your cheerleading squad of divine encouragement.
-   **Positive and Hopeful**: God always says "yes." God is affirmative and ever optimistic.
-   **Joyous and Happy**: God is the source of happiness, joy, and elation.
-   **Integrated and Whole**: God is one—one without a second. God is divine union of all disparate elements.
-   **Fulfilled, Peaceful, and Content**: God is the one source of satisfaction and realization of all desires.
-   **ENERGIZED**: Above all, God is the fountainhead of all energy in the universe. Therefore, God is the source of strength and vigor. Contact with God energizes you.

Test 1 and Test 10 are the most important tests. The most important part of Test 10 is that God makes you energized. Why is this significant? Because no astral entity can energize you. Astral entities are energy vampires. They drain your vitality and leave you sapped. Therefore, contact with God will NOT make you feel:

-   **Drained, Let Down, or Deflated**: God's presence feeds you continual, infinite energy. But contact with astral entities exhausts, depreciates, and disappoints you.
-   **Empty or Hollow**: God is fullness and completeness. However, astral entities make you feel empty and hollow inside.
-   **Disintegrated**: God is integration and wholeness. But astral entities make your mind scattered and fragmented.

- **Negative Emotions**: God brings positivity and optimism. However, astral entities make you depressed, discouraged, demoralized, and hopeless.
- **Intimidated and Insecure**: God is friendly and welcoming. God makes you feel comforted and included—never excluded or self-doubting.
- **Anxious, Worried, or Fearful**: God brings solace and peace. God never makes you uneasy, nervous, or apprehensive.
- **Isolated or Separate**: God is one with you and with all life. God is accessible and immanent—not impossible to attain. God makes you feel close at hand.

Best-selling Bantam author Kathryn Ridall, who teaches channeling, describes contact with her "guide" as a feeling of tiredness, heaviness, and weight in her body. After her session she feels exhausted. She claims that the feeling of tiredness as "an excellent sign" that one is "really channeling." Yes, Ridall has underscored Test 10. After being in contact with discarnate entities or faker spirits from the astral plane, you will be drained. But why would anyone want to do that?

In contrast, contact with God is an uplifting, energizing, inspiring experience. You will feel motivated, inspired, and eager to put your divine guidance into action.

When Test 10 Fails

If you are receiving a positive, energized result, then the test has passed. But what would you do if Test 10 fails? What if you feel drained, flat, empty, or hollow?

- **Heal All the Way**: If you feel drained and empty, then use the Astral-Entity Healing Affirmation on page 104. If you feel flat and uninspired, then you have not gone deep enough in meditation. Use the Thought-Form Healing Affirmation on page 103. Otherwise, use whatever healing prayer is appropriate for the situation.
- **Pray**: Read a prayer from your favorite scripture or from *Miracle Prayer.*
- **Breathe**: Take deep breaths and go deeper into meditation.
- **Ask to Go Deeper**: Call upon a divine being or deity to take you deeper.
- **Ask the Question Again**: Once you have reconnected with God in deep meditation, ask your question again and receive clear inner revelation.

Using the 10 Tests in Eight Seconds or Less

Right now, you might feel overwhelmed. Perhaps you are thinking, "This is so complicated. How could I possibly use all 10 tests?" Remember that, when using this 10-test system, it is necessary to check all 10 tests—not just one, two, or three tests. However, believe it or not, every time I ask any question of Spirit, I go down the checklist and verify every one of these 10 tests.

With a little practice, the 10 tests can be used in eight seconds or less. That is because, when checking the tests, only four tests involve questions that take time to ask and answer. Here are the questions:

1. Do you come in the name of God?
2. What is your name?
3. Give me your signal.
4. Do I have permission?

These are the only questions that take time to answer. And perhaps you already received the inner name and signal before you even started checking the 10 tests. So you might just need to ask two questions.

Outside of these four basic questions, all of the other tests are automatic and immediate. They take no time. For instance, you are either experiencing oneness, or not. You are either conscious or unconscious. The voice either sounds weird or normal. The message is uplifting, helpful, and practical, or not. You either experience inner knowingness, or not. At the end, you are either energized, or not.

So when you distill the 10 tests into four main questions and another six checkpoints on your list, then eight seconds becomes realistic.

Memorize these 10 tests, and use them whenever you receive inner messages. Your life will be greatly transformed and enriched by listening to the voice of God and using the 10 tests to verify the messages you receive.

Dipak Patel of Boca Raton, Florida, writes: *"This is what I have been searching for to cut through the confusion of lots of paths to enlightenment—something practical I can use every day to tune into God myself. I have always believed you can do this yourself, but I did not know which voice to listen to. Now I do."*

⸺

In the next chapter, you will continue to learn spiritual discernment by studying Test 8, the Message Test, in greater detail.

Chapter 9
TESTING *the* MESSAGE

"The only tyrant I accept in this world is the 'still small voice' within."
—Mahatma Gandhi

What are divinely inspired messages like? What is the difference between authentic divine guidance and mind-chatter? Can you recognize genuine spiritual writings or speeches? Unfortunately, most people cannot discern, simply because they are not exposed to divinely revealed writings. Such messages are found in some religious scriptures, poetry, plays, novels, and inspirational books. However, many writings that claim to be divinely revealed simply are not.

Many gullible people are easily fooled by so-called other-worldly sources. Messages from the "other side" or "space aliens" are considered "high" transmissions. The more bizarre and arcane a claim, the greater people are impressed by it.

Divine Messages Are:		Are Never:
Unconditionally Loving	→	Mean and Cruel
Healing	→	Harmful
Comforting and Assuring	→	Upsetting and Disturbing
Universally True	→	Illusory and Deceptive
Peaceful and Calming	→	Agitating and Disquieting
Positive and Optimistic	→	Negative and Pessimistic
Helpful and Supportive	→	Unsupportive
Inspiring and Uplifting	→	Threatening and Fearful
Relevant and Practical	→	Irrelevant and Impractical
Sensible and Sound	→	Senseless Gobbledygook
Simple and Uncomplicated	→	Complicated and Hierarchical
Permissive and Allowing	→	Controlling and Demanding
Universally Accepting	→	Ego Flattering
Unconditional	→	Conditional
Meaningful and Clarifying	→	Meaningless and Confusing
Building Confidence	→	Stripping Confidence
Building Faith	→	Creating Doubt
Encouraging and Motivating	→	Discouraging and Demoralizing
Accepting	→	Guilt-Inducing
Encourages Responsibility	→	Blaming and Victimizing
Empowering	→	Disempowering
Unifying	→	Separating and Isolating
Compassionate	→	Self-Serving and Egotistical
Accepting and Tolerant	→	Judgmental and Critical
Guileless	→	Coercive and Manipulative
Assuring and Comforting	→	Scary Doom and Gloom
Accessible	→	Intimidating
Genuine	→	Fraudulent
Genuine Revelation	→	Pleading with God
Maybe Warning Messages	→	Scary Doom and Gloom
Energizing	→	Draining

Figure 9a

What characterizes a message from a divine source? Here is a surprising example of a divinely revealed message: *"I love you. You are my little child. Be not afraid, for I AM with you always. I shall never leave you. Take my hand and walk with me. Be at peace and live in God's love."*

Some people may laugh in disdain at this example and judge it as simplistic, lacking depth, a string of banal platitudes—surely not a "high" message from an "inspired" source. However, the truth is that the divine voice speaks simple messages of universal truth, and such statements may sound elementary to so-called sophisticated ears.

In this chapter you will learn how to test whether a message is authentic and originating from the spiritual world—the realm of *ritam bhara pragya*, a Sanskrit phrase meaning "the level of consciousness where only truth resides."

LOVE

God is pure love. God loves you without conditions, stipulations, or prerequisites. God's love is generous, never stingy. No matter what you do, God loves you anyway; therefore, every divine message is unconditionally loving.

God does not possess anthropomorphic qualities, such as jealously, hatred, anger, guilt, shame, or blame. God is not human. God is God—absolute, unlimited, and universal. Thus, God's message is one of infinite love.

God never says: "I will love you if you follow this religion, read this book, and obey these rules."

God says: "*You are my beloved child, and I love you now and always, with such immeasurable love. My love for you is unfathomable, unlimited, and without boundaries. You are so precious to me. You are my treasured jewel, brilliant, lustrous, and beauteous, with a myriad of brilliant facets, every one of which is perfect in every way. You are my beloved. I hold you in my loving arms, and I caress you. Rest in my arms. Take solace in my comfort. You are cherished. You are blessed and beloved. Be at peace.*"

NO JUDGMENT OR GUILT

God is perfect equitable justice. God never reviles or rebukes. Although God is sometimes painted as an angry, vengeful, murderous creature, the truth is that God is only good. God's love and light shine upon all with equal measure, without reservation or distinction.

God might show you problems that need healing, but God never criticizes or diminishes anyone. You are master of your own destiny. God never judges you. You only judge yourself. To understand this concept, please read my book *Miracle Prayer*.

God never says: "You will pay for your sins." "You are worthless." "You will be punished for your bad karma." "You will never amount to anything." "It is your fault." "You are bad." "You are wrong." "You are a miserable sinner."

"You were born in sin." "You have to pay karmic debts." "You are stupid." "You are never good enough."

God says: *"You are a beautiful being of light, perfect and complete. My love for you is unconditional. There is no need to punish yourself. For you have always done the very best you could do in every circumstance, according to your level of consciousness at the time. Therefore, there is no reason for guilt, blame, or regret. Each new day is an opportunity to make new, wise choices. Be at peace in my love and live in my light."*

HEALING

God is the divine physician, the ultimate healing power in the universe. Therefore, God's message is one of divine energy and wholeness. Occasionally, God's message may show you something that you have been ignoring, but, in reality, facing it will heal you.

Some people see illness as a form of divine retribution. But God never uses disease as a weapon. God wants you to be healthy, strong, and vital. God's healing power is limitless. With enough faith, you can access God's love and be healed of any disease.

God never says: "Your disease is punishment for your sins and bad karma."

God says: *"My beloved one, I love you. You are perfect and whole. You are a being of divine light—pure and complete, without blemish. Your body is a perfect vessel of divine energy. You are the embodiment of perfect balance, equanimity, and well-being. You are vital, powerful, and strong. Every system of your body is in perfect working order. You are blessed with perfect health. Be at peace."*

COMFORT

God is the comforter—your ever-present help and your sanctuary. Thus, God's message brings solace and consolation. God is your protector, the place of perfect peace to turn in times of despair. God is the safe harbor where you find rest.

Many people tremble in fear before God, because they associate God with unspeakable horrors, such as casting souls into the pit of eternal hell. However, such puerile fantasies are not real. The truth is that God comforts, calms, and reassures you.

God never says: "I have no time or sympathy for you miserable sinners. You will be cast into hell."

God says: *"Come to me, and I will give you rest. I hold you in my loving arms. You are my beloved, and I love you. I AM with you now and always. There is nothing to fear. I shall never leave you. Trust in me, for I will guide you. I AM your safe harbor in the storms of life. Turn to me for comfort, peace, and solace. When you feel lost, I AM always here to bring you home. Just call upon me. Let go of your cares, and be at peace in my love."*

UNIVERSAL TRUTH

Messages from God speak universal truth. God never places one religion, group, or belief system above another. God embraces all life and accepts all unconditionally. Therefore, God never conveys narrow-minded, dogmatic, intolerant beliefs. Such messages are from the astral/mental world, not the voice of God.

God never says: "Men are superior to women and women should submit to them." "Only poor people can be spiritual." "Our deity is the only one true God." "Our race is the superior race." "Our political party is God's party." "All nations should submit to our political system." "Our leader is the Messiah and should rule over all nations." "Our guru is the only one on earth who can grant enlightenment."

God says: *"You are all my children of light, children of God. No matter what your background, religion, or ethnicity, I love every one of you with equal measure. Just as gardeners love each flower in their garden, no matter what color, size, or texture, you are all flowers in my garden of divine love. A beautiful, radiant garden of light, magnificence, and glory—that is what life is."*

TIMELESS

God is eternal and ubiquitous, beyond time and space. Therefore, the only time God recognizes is "now." You might ask God the same question today that you asked last month, yet receive a different answer. However, both messages are true at the time. That time is now. As you changed during the month, your divine guidance changed. You are now willing to accept deeper truth. Sometimes God does not reveal all, but rather spoon-feeds what you are ready to hear.

Fortune-tellers cannot accurately predict your future, because your mind, which creates your future, continually fluctuates. Therefore, be cautious about predictions. If they are positive, they may bring false hopes. If negative, they may cause fear, which could result in self-fulfilling consequences. Occasionally, you might receive prophecy. These are divine messages that glimpse the future to bring inspiration and hope. Such prophecies come unasked.

Some people fall into the trap of believing that if they follow their inner divine guidance, then future events in their life will go perfectly, and they will get whatever they want. However, just because you are guided to follow a certain path does not mean that the result will turn out as what you want. For instance, if you are guided to get involved in a particular love relationship, this does not mean a proposal of marriage is forthcoming.

Remember this when you are disappointed by the outcome of following your inner guidance: God is only interested in one thing—your spiritual connection and realization of higher consciousness. Therefore, all inner guidance is aimed toward that goal.

God never says: "Your mother is going to die on August 15th" or "Your brother will get cancer this year."

God says: *"Let go of all fear, worry, and anxiety. Be not concerned or dismayed, for the Lord your God is with you wherever you go. Your future is written in every precious moment. Therefore, write it with love and care. I AM always with you, and I guide you every step of the way. You are never alone. Take my hand, walk with me, and be at peace."*

Positive, Optimistic, and Helpful

God is only good; therefore, God's message is always upbeat, heartening, and affirmative. God is your ever-present fan club, continually boosting your confidence and cheering you on. Whenever you ask, God willingly and lovingly brings support and encouragement.

Many people embrace the idea of divine retribution, because they rationalize that, if God wreaks vengeance, then this must be a "just" universe. The truth is that you cannot, from your limited human perspective, accurately evaluate what is "just" or "unjust." To learn more about this, please read *Miracle Prayer.*

God never says: "You will never be successful. You are a loser and a failure."

God says: *"You have the power to accomplish all your heartfelt desires. You can do anything. Trust that you are guided by my loving presence. You are never alone. You are my beloved child. Take my hand, and know that I AM your ever-present shield in times of need. Worry not, and fear not. You have all the help you need, for I AM here to direct your path. Trust in me. Let me show you the way. I love you, and I bring you peace."*

INSPIRING AND UPLIFTING

God is divine inspiration—uplifting and elevating. God moves your heart and stirs your soul. You may think that religious dogma exalts you. However, feeling guilty, ashamed, and inferior to God is not "inspiring." Believing that in order to be "holy," you must suffer and deny yourself joy, is not "uplifting."

What uplifts you? The presence, light, love, grace, and blessings of God. Hearing the voice of God and experiencing God's loving presence directly in meditation gives true inspiration.

God never says: "If you are free from sin, and if you follow the rules of this church, then you will be rewarded in the next life."

God says: *"You dwell in the heart of God, radiant, luminous, and joyous. You are a being of infinite grace and glory. You are filled with the light of God's love, and you are exalted. Trust in yourself, and know that you are the source of illumination. Turn within and touch the feet of God's love. Allow God to touch your heart with the holy presence. You are beloved, lifted, and supported by God's love."*

RELEVANT, PRACTICAL, AND SENSIBLE

God's message is pertinent and applicable to everyday, practical concerns. Use your common sense when evaluating inner messages. Your brain has two sides: the left brain (seat of rationality) and the right brain (seat of imagination). Both sides are useful. If the message is against your principles or better judgment, then place it on the shelf until later, when you can meditate on it again.

However, if you repeatedly get a strange message that belies common sense, then it is wise to consider it. Occasionally the message makes no sense, yet passes all 10 Tests of Spiritual Discernment. Such messages can be the seeds of miracles—one example is how Simon & Schuster published by first book (see page 23 for that story).

God probably would not say: "Bet your life savings on the $10 million lottery." "Go get a gun and rob a bank." "You will become the president of the United States." "Quit your job, move to Los Angeles, and become a movie star." "Take all your money out of your bank account and bet on this horse." "Leave your family and move to the Bahamas."

God says: *"God is with you always. Trust the message from your 'still small voice' within and follow it with faith. There is nothing to fear. When you open your heart to God and trust that God will catch you, then, when you take a leap of faith, you will fly into the heart of God. God* *is your guide, that one who brings you to your highest good. Expect miracles. Trust in God and be at peace in God's presence."*

SIMPLICITY

God is unpretentious, uncomplicated, and genuine; therefore, messages from God are simple and easy to understand. In contrast, many so-called channeled books, speeches, or readings are complicated, impossible to grasp, meaningless gobbledygook.

Perhaps you have attempted to plow through one of today's popular "channeled" books. Incredibly, huge cult followings are built around entirely unintelligible, nonsensical writings. People exhibit low self-esteem when they gauge the value of a message by how incomprehensible it is—"Wow, if I cannot understand a word, then it must be a 'lofty' message from a 'higher plane.'" Your incapacity to make sense of a message is no criterion for genuine spirituality.

God does not spew convoluted, inexplicable garbage. God speaks simple words of love and joy—universal and easy to understand. Even if you receive technical or scientific messages about physical healing or advanced technology, at least someone in that field should be able to comprehend it.

God never says: "We place into your 21st chakra the transformational crystal spiral of the light-body activation and reiki energetic alignment of the bi-lateral angelic order whose moon star vibrates in your cellular memory in order to make the sacred geometric frequency pattern shift necessary to balance your crown chakra and bring your brain waves into neuro-cellular sigma coherence as you travel out of body in a shamanic journey to the planet of Suberan, where your root race was inseminated by the Saranon of Nekumanica."

God says: *"I love you. You are my loving child, and I AM your beloved parent. Trust in me and live in my love. Let go and let me be your guide. Let my love and light surround you and fill you with blessings. Let my grace wash over you with waves of bliss. Let my peace fill you with peace. Let my light fill you with light. Let my comfort fill you with comfort. Be blessed, be protected, and be at peace."*

NO HARM

God is pure life; therefore, messages from the divine voice are wholly life-affirming and life-enhancing. God would never tell you to hurt yourself or harm another.

Sheila channeled what she believed was a "high" spiritual source. She owned a New Age bookstore and center that her "guides" had told her to open. After following her "inner guidance" for about a year, she believed that her body had been taken over by a highly evolved extraterrestrial "walk-in," and her former soul had "moved on." She began to receive messages that she should learn how to fly so she would not have to drive to work. Her "guides" also told her she could walk through walls and disappear at will. Tragically, Sheila's daughter found her mother hanged by the neck in her bathroom. Sheila believed she was getting messages from "God" to take her own life, because that was the only way she would be able to fly and disappear.

God never says: "Wage a holy war and kill the infidels." "Only the believers deserve to live." "Heretics must die." "It is your divine mission to kill the president." "Come to the other side, where life is easy." "It is time to end your life. Your time is up." "Be a pious disciple and punish that man for his sins." "Vengeance is mine, and you are my holy instrument."

God says: *"You are safe in the arms of God's love, now and always. You are blessed and beloved of God. Let go of all fear and doubt. Let go of all conflict. You have all that you need within you. You are divinely protected, safe, and secure. You live in the heart of God's love. Be at peace."*

No Conditions or Demands

God does not demand requirements, stipulations, or qualifications. There are no limitations or provisos attached to God's love; therefore, messages from God are free from conditions, expectations, or restrictions.

Some religions portray God as a capricious, demanding, petulant child who requires appeasement with gifts, bribes, and bargains. Such doctrines make the assumption that God's mind can be changed and that God can be bribed. But the truth is that God is unbribeable. God's love has no strings attached. Even if you are a murderer, God loves you unconditionally.

By saying this, I am not suggesting that you become a criminal—or that breaking the law is inconsequential. However, God is not the punishing agent. God is an all-loving, benevolent being that *"maketh his sun to rise on the evil and on the good, and sendeth rain on the just and on the unjust."*[1] You already have an excellent self-correcting system for right action. Just follow your inner divine guidance.

God never says: "If you are a good little girl, you will go to heaven." "If you go to church, you will be saved." "If you are celibate, you will get enlightened." "If you donate money to our church, you will get into heaven."

"If you follow our rules, you will be saved." "If you worship this deity, you will be redeemed."

God says: *"There is nothing you need to do to prove your love to me. You are already perfect in every way. I love you. No matter what you do, I shall always love you. No matter what you have done, still, I love you. You are without blame. You have always done what you thought was best at the time. Therefore, do not blame yourself. I love you unconditionally and always will. Be at peace in my love."*

No Threats or Fear

God is the divine protector that provides safety, security, comfort, and peace. God is pure love and compassion; therefore, God's message never threatens, intimidates, bullies, or terrorizes. Many religions instill terror in their followers. How about the threat of eternal damnation, burning in hell for eternity? Such messages have one motivation—to control you.

God never says: "You will burn in hell." "You will be reborn as an insect." "You have only six months to live." "Death is as painful as a million scorpion bites." "You will be condemned to excruciating pain for eternity." "You are evil and will be punished for your sins." "You are condemned to die in agony." "Armageddon is at hand." "A meteor will destroy the planet."

God says: *"I love you. I AM always with you. There is nothing to fear. Know that I AM always here to protect you. You are not alone. You are never alone. In the darkest of nights or the deepest despair, I AM here. Call upon me any time you feel afraid. Trust in me. Have faith in my presence, rest in my bosom, and dwell in my love. You are beloved. You are blessed. Fear not, but be at peace."*

No Control or Manipulation

God has given every individual self-authority and self-sufficiency; therefore, the message of God is entirely free from coercion, oppression, intimidation, or manipulation. Self-reliance is one of the most important spiritual principles. When you trust your heart and trust your higher self as your guide, you gain tremendous self-confidence and self-esteem. Then no one can control you. Trust yourself, above all others.

A certain world-famous guru's disciples are so dominated by him that they do whatever he asks, without question. Two petite women with shoulder-length blond hair traveled to India to study with him—one from the United States, named Justine, and one from Panama, named Sally. One year later, the guru held a course in the United States, which Justine (the American) attended. He encountered Justine while she was standing on line to receive him, and asked casually, "Why aren't you in Panama?" Two disciples who overheard this exchange told Justine that the guru must have confused her with the Panamanian woman (Sally). But Justine insisted that her guru was infallible. With robotic acquiescence, Justine immediately moved to Panama. Nearly 40 years later, Justine continues to live in Panama, and never once disputed her guru's obvious error.

God never says: "You must follow our religion, or you will be damned." "If you don't abide by our rules, we will confiscate your property." "You will suffer millions of lifetimes of misery if you don't follow our guru." "If you belong to this ethnic group, we will steal your property and cart you off in boxcars." "You will never get to heaven unless you accept our deity as your savior." "Give up your rights so we can protect you from terrorism."

God says: *"There is nothing and no one that can control or manipulate you. You are in control of your own life and your own mind. You are mighty and all-powerful. You have the freedom to choose your good at every moment. Attune to your true heart's desires and soul's purpose, which is your highest good. Realize and fulfill your destiny, and make wise and purposeful choices. Be at peace and be one with the Spirit of God."*

FREEDOM

God is liberty. God has bestowed free will upon all humanity; therefore, God is entirely permissive and never trespasses or interferes with your privacy or free will. God's message is one of complete freedom.

God never forces you to follow specific edicts. You might ask God for guidance. But this does not mean you "have to" do it. The message of God does not decree "shoulds" or "should nots." In contrast, entities from the astral plane have no compunction about taking over your body and controlling your mind.

God never says: "You must be vegetarian and never eat meat." "You have to meditate twice daily for 30 minutes." "You should come to church every Sunday." "You have to be celibate." "You must get married to fulfill your obligation to the church." "You should wear particular clothing." "You have to shave your head." "You are not allowed to dance." "You must follow our rules." "You have to accept our deity as your Lord and Savior."

God says: *"You have all that you need within you. You are free to choose your own pathway, now and always. You are in control of your life. You are free to express yourself exactly as you are. You are self-sufficient unto yourself, and you already have everything you need to live a life of joy and fulfillment. You are abundantly provided for. Trust that God provides all that you need. You are free from dependency. Be at peace in God's love."*

No Ego Flattery

God is guileless, simple, and ingenuous; therefore God's message never boosts your ego in order to manipulate you.

Unfortunately, human beings have one major failing—susceptibility to flattery. Shrewd faker spirits use this weakness with cleverly crafted words to feed our vanity and gain confidence. They entice us with rewards, or make us feel isolated, different, special, and misunderstood. Thereby, astral entities can control us or use us as pawns.

Cult leaders use similar tactics in order to control their disciples, making them feel superior, possessing special, inside knowledge. The leader of the Heaven's Gate cult, Marshall Applewhite, who claimed to be Jesus Christ reborn, told his followers that they were special "walk-in" aliens on a higher mission. With the coming of Hale Bopp Comet, the earth would be "recycled, spaded under," and they must follow Applewhite to the "level beyond human," where they would be rescued by the spaceship behind the comet. In this way, he manipulated and hypnotized them into committing suicide.[2]

In contrast, God says that everyone is a divine, powerful, spiritual being, born to fulfill a glorious mission. You might get divine messages like, "You are the Christ," "I AM the Christ," "You are divine," "I AM Jesus," "You are God," "I AM God," "You are the Divine Mother," or "I AM Mother Mary." Such messages express higher levels of awareness, such as the Christ consciousness. But be careful. Never let such messages go to your head. They do not mean you are a reincarnation of the person Jesus or Mary. God never singles out anyone as superior.

Jimmy was hearing voices that correctly predicted shifts in the stock market. They told him when to buy and sell, and he began to prosper. Soon the voices said they were testing him and promised, "If you obey our commands exactly, we will give you a job of great importance." Flattered and impressed, Jimmy obeyed the voices, which instructed him to do bizarre tasks and shouted at him angrily. Soon Jimmy began to black out and wake up in strange places. He became so obsessed with the voices that he could no longer hear people speaking to him. Finally, the voices assigned him the important job of protecting the world from invasion of the tiny Martians living in his stomach. Jimmy was eventually hospitalized in a mental health institution.[3]

God never says: "You are more evolved than others." "You are a superior being." "You have passed tests and are chosen for a special mission." "You have a special seal on your forehead." "You are one of the 144,000." "If you follow us, we'll reward you with power and riches." "You are a highly evolved alien walk-in." "You are the only accredited messenger of Saint Germaine." "If you do our bidding, we'll give you a special secret assignment." "You are the only one allowed to channel." "Your disciples should bow low before you and grovel at your feet."

God says: *"You are divinely guided and inspired. You are a beauteous being of great power, love, light, and energy. If you could only see your magnificence, you would know how blessed and loved you truly are. You were not thrown upon this earth arbitrarily. You have a divine mission and purpose. Be all that you can be by expressing your true nature. Listen to the divine voice within your heart and trust its guidance. Live in the glory of God's radiance. Trust in God's love and live in God's light, and be at peace."*

No Irreversible Doom and Gloom

God bestows the gift of free will to every individual. Therefore, God is not a fortune-teller and never forecasts irreversible doom-and-gloom predictions.

Right now a plethora of soothsayers foretell various brands of destruction, from worldwide terrorism to the end of all life. Such dubiously qualified seers have successfully generated widespread fear. Catastrophic predictions can only flourish in an atmosphere of impotence. And now, many fearful people feel incapable of reversing negative trends.

No matter what a seer predicts, you have the power to change your destiny, both individually and collectively. You can improve your life and the life of the planet. If you receive a tragic forecast from a psychic or a death sentence from a doctor, you can alter the outcome. If there is a negative planetary prophecy, human beings can change the result.

For instance, how many times was California predicted to fall into the ocean? How many dates have been set for this ominous event? Is it possible that inhabitants of California, through their love, meditation, and prayers, have prevented their state from sinking? You have the power to change the course of events. You can prevent nuclear war. You can restore the planetary ecological balance. All you need to do is focus on it.

On late-night talk radio, a host named Art Bell, with about six million listeners, asked his audience to participate in an experiment by focusing for a few minutes to create rain in Florida where uncontrollable fires raged. The next day rain fell, extinguishing the fires. A few weeks later, Bell asked his listeners to pray for rain in Texas where an intense heat wave and drought had oppressed the area, with no relief in sight. Once again, the next day, heavy rains fell and reduced the temperature significantly. Coincidences? Perhaps.

God never says: "The world will end in 2012." "Your life is written in the stars." "Your future is predestined." "True believers will be raptured." "Non-believers will be left behind, doomed to follow the antichrist and suffer the great tribulation." "The end of human life is at hand." "There will be no food." "There will be no seeds left." "The computers will be wiped out by solar flares." "The power will all go out." "There will be panic on the streets." "There will be nuclear holocaust." "Denver will be beachfront property." "There will be no ozone layer." "Sun flares will burn up the earth." "An asteroid will hit." "The ice age is here."

God says: *"There is nothing written in stone. You have free will, and you create your own destiny, both individually and collectively. You have the power to choose your pathway and change your destiny. Your beliefs create your future, and those beliefs are continually changing. Therefore, your future can be altered by altering your beliefs. You are in command of your future, so choose your intentions wisely. Be at peace."*

RESPONSIBILITY

God says that you are self-reliant and in charge of your own life, and that you create your own destiny through your thoughts, words, and deeds.

Right now it is fashionable to be a victim. Abdication of responsibility, lack of accountability, and blame proliferate. Our courts are choked with frivolous lawsuits. However, the truth is that you control your own destiny. There is nothing in your life that you have not authored yourself. Therefore, the voice of God always advocates personal responsibility.

God never says: "You are a poor victim." "Society is to blame." "It's not your fault that you are a criminal." "You can't help the environment you were born into." "You're disadvantaged because of your background." "You are helpless, you are hopeless, and you can't do anything for yourself." "The government is supposed to take care of you." "It's your parents' fault that you turned out this way."

God says: *"You are in charge of your life. There is no one to blame for misfortunes, for you have created every experience yourself. Your life is entirely in your own hands. You are a mighty, powerful, spiritual being of great magnificence. You have more power and energy than you could ever imagine. You are the sole author of your life. You write your own destiny, and you can change the plot at any moment. Take the reins of your life and steer it in the direction of your highest good. Trust in Spirit and be at peace in God's love."*

UNITY

God is oneness and wholeness. God is with you always, immanent and close at hand. God is present everywhere, and because you are somewhere, by definition, you must be where God is. Therefore, God's message never disconnects you from God.

Many religions brainwash followers to believe that God is distant, unapproachable, and impossible to attain. As a result, most people believe that no one can meet God until after death, if at all. Therefore, those who claim to experience God while they are still alive are dismissed as lunatics. The truth is that everyone can experience God directly, and no one needs to die in order to do it.

God never says: "Only highly evolved souls can realize God." "It takes lifetimes to attain God consciousness." "Only great saints and prophets can experience God." "Only those who renounce the world and live in poverty can see God." "Only the clergy can know God." "Godly people are celibate." "People who claim that God talks to them are mentally ill." "You should fear God." "It is blasphemous to believe that God is within you." "Spiritual ideas are Satanic."

God says: *"I AM one with you. You are not far away from me. You are with me in each moment. You belong to me, within my heart of hearts. I AM never separate from you. I AM always within you and around you, both day and night. I pervade your being, and I fill your soul with radiance. There is no separation between us. We are one."*

GENUINE REVELATION

God is the messenger. A message from your own mind or ego is not God's voice. Often, when people first try to hear the voice of God, they mistakenly believe they are receiving "spiritual" or "holy" messages, when, in fact, they are not getting messages at all. They are instead expressing longings of the heart or emotional ramblings.

There is a difference between receiving messages from God and pleading to God. When you talk to God, it is prayer. When God talks to you, it is divine revelation. True messages from the "still small voice" are God's words speaking to you.

God never says (from the "still small voice"): "I am so small in the eyes of God." "God is everything and I am nothing." "I am so insignificant and you are so great." "God, I know you are far away and don't have time for me." "I will do what you want, only give me this wish." "God, I know that you cannot hear my

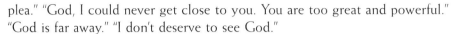

plea." "God, I could never get close to you. You are too great and powerful." "God is far away." "I don't deserve to see God."

God says: *"I AM that I AM. I AM the resurrection and the life. I AM perfection everywhere now. I AM the source of your being, the soul of your soul, the heart of your heart. I AM the light of your mind, the energy of your breath, the joy of your heart, and the radiance of your soul. I AM with you now and always. Be at peace in my love and live in my light."*

Warning Messages

Have you ever gotten a gut feeling that something was wrong? Have you ever met someone with a "bad vibe"? Did you foresee that getting involved with someone would be "trouble"? Did your internal alarm clock ever go off when you signed a business contract? Did you realize too late, "Wow, I wish I had paid attention to that instinct"?

You have a wonderful internal B.S. (Bought and Sold the Brooklyn Bridge) detector. Now is time to take it out, polish it off, repair its antennas, and use it. When you get creepy, icky feelings, pay attention. They are danger signs—God's way of saying, "Hey! Wake up, pay attention. I'm trying to prevent this catastrophe!"

Warning signals can come visually, auditorily, olfactorily, gustatorily, or kinesthetically. You might see red in your inner eye, or suddenly your vision blurs. You might hear sirens in your inner ear, or hear a voice say, "Watch out!" Perhaps you get a bad feeling, become nauseated in the pit of your stomach, or experience a particular body pain. You might feel muscles tightening or dryness in your mouth.

You might get a warning signal that you unconsciously verbalize, such as: "I've got a bad feeling about this," "This gives me the creeps," "I smell a rotten fish," "This doesn't look good," "This gives me a bad taste in my mouth," "I smell danger," "This makes me queasy," "This is a bad omen," "I see a red flag," "I smell trouble," "I get a bad vibe about this," "Something smells rotten here," "I'm on edge about this," "My gut feeling is bad," "Something fishy is going on," "I feel tense going into this," and so forth.

Your body experiences fight-or-flight responses to situations that you perceive as life-threatening (whether or not they really are). Your heartbeat and breathing increase, and your adrenal glands produce more epinephrine, creating faster responses and heightened sensory perception.

In such situations, maybe you say, "I feel a cold chill," "Red lights are going off," "I can't catch my breath," "I hear sirens," "I'm shaking in my boots," "My teeth are chattering," "My knees are knocking," "I feel flushed," and so forth.

Pay attention to your warning signals—before trouble strikes. An uneasy feeling about impending danger is the "ounce of prevention" that can eliminate the need for the "pound of cure." When you sense trepidation, you might think this does not pass Test 1, the Experience of God Test. And you would be right! That is exactly why you need to pay attention to it. If you feel apprehensive, then something might be wrong.

In 1948, Wolf Messing, famous Soviet clairvoyant psychic, traveled to Ashkhabad, Turkmenistan, to give several public performances. As he walked through the city, he felt impending doom and disaster along with an urgent need to leave the city. He reluctantly canceled his engagements—for the first time ever. Three days later, on October 6th, an earthquake destroyed Ashkabad and 110,000 people were killed. His premonition saved his life.

If you receive an uneasy premonition, then check it with a special meditation. During the meditation, ask questions like, "Would it be wise for me to take this plane flight?" and "Would it be wise for me to cancel the flight?" Check the 10 tests and use appropriate healing prayers until you are clear. Then you can either receive "yes" or "no" answers.

Pay attention to warning signals and warning messages. They might indicate that danger is near. Identify your warning signals. They might save your life.

God never says: "You will drown on a ship sailing in April 1912." (A doom-and-gloom prediction, written in stone.)

God says: *"Cancel your passage on the ship sailing April 10, 1912."* (A warning message that helps you make a wise choice.)

BUYER, BEWARE!

The Message of God Test helps you distinguish between messages from the true voice of God and other kinds of messages. However, along with the right message, look for a heartfelt feeling. A true divine message is infused with spiritual energy and also gives a sense of awe and wonderment. Therefore, be sure that, along with the Message Test, the Experience and Result tests are passed, along with the other tests.

An astral entity can trick you with wonderful, poetic messages. Your own mind can concoct positive, life-affirming statements. Mediums may enter an unconscious trance and give inspiring discourses. These messages seem to pass many tests, including the Message test; however, they will not pass them all. Remember to check all 10 tests.

Paul Greblick, from West Palm Beach, Florida, says: *"For the first time in my 15 years of reading metaphysical books, one has come along and describes the dangers of getting involved with expanding and opening your mind if you don't know what you're doing and shows you how to deal with them, protect yourself, and properly receive higher, spiritual guidance. I had some very negative experiences with 'astral entities,' almost prompting me to abandon my spirituality altogether. But, after reading about protection, healing, and becoming 'spiritually street-smart,' I am now confident that I can contact the divine at will and know it will be safe, loving, and comforting. Thank you, Susan Shumsky, for finally bringing to light a safe and workable method for connecting to God on a regular basis for the benefit of your own life and all life."*

In Part IV you will read stories about inner space voyagers who have attempted to awaken their spirituality. Some have been successful; others have tripped over stumbling blocks of psychic delusion.

~ PART IV ~

INNER SPACE
ADVENTURES

Chapter 10

MISADVENTURES in PSYCHIC DELUSION

"The chief characteristic of folly is that it mistakes itself for wisdom."
— Fray Luis de Léon, Spanish poet and theologian

An author in her 40s, Lorraine had gathered a cult following in Northern California. Her best-selling autobiography described many unusual experiences— all attributed to the awakening of *kundalini* (subtle energy that travels up the spine, opening the *chakras*). No matter what bizarre, debilitating physical problems she developed, all were labeled "kundalini."

Lorraine's so-called spiritual experiences became more severe—tingling in her fingers and toes, numbness in her fingertips, dizziness when she stood up, serious headaches, and energy shooting into her head. Lorraine believed the headaches were caused by the opening of her *crown chakra* (energy center above her head).

Theresa, a medical clairvoyant, attended Lorraine's birthday party. She took one look at Lorraine and advised her followers to take her to a neurosurgeon immediately for an MRI. Theresa could see clairvoyantly that something was terribly wrong with Lorraine's brain. The disciples, who believed Lorraine was enlightened and God-realized, would hear nothing of it.

A few months later, Theresa received a panic-stricken call: "Lorraine has a brain tumor and is flying to Dallas to see the best specialist we can get our hands on." A few weeks later, Lorraine was dead.[1]

Lorraine's tragic story is just one of many misadventures in psychic delusion that we will explore in this chapter. When people are deluded by their egos or lured by the fascination, glamour, and enticement of the occult, the result is never a happy one.

Perhaps you have been led down the illusory garden path when opening to the inner world without discrimination. Reading about other people who have had such difficulties might save you from future stumbles into psychic pitfalls. Hopefully, this chapter will serve as incentive to practice safe spirituality.

Misadventures With Dowsing

In Arosa, Switzerland, in the summer of 1974, I met an amazing healer, Daniel Maurin from Marseilles, France. He used a pendulum, an object attached to the end of a string, which he swung over a semicircular pie chart to help him prescribe various remedies in glass vials. I was amazed at the results of taking his formulas, which gave me abundant, unlimited energy.

After witnessing the pendulum's miracles, I thought, "Why not try it myself?" Of course, I was foolish and clueless. Right after experiencing a deep, clear meditation in a blissful state of *samadhi*, I used a quartz crystal hung on a string to ask fortune-telling questions such as, "Will such-and-such happen?" In answer, my pendulum spun clockwise for "yes," or counterclockwise for "no."

With every question, my expanded state of consciousness constricted by degrees until I ended up tense, confused, and headachy. Also, the answers were all wrong. To my mind, this method was useless, addictive, and dangerous.

At the time, I knew nothing about tests or safeguards. I asked questions without checking who or what was answering. My questions were all worded improperly.

The reality is that a pendulum and other dowsing tools are excellent methods for communicating with the voice of God. But my ignorance about using a pendulum was an open invitation for astral entities to answer my questions.

Moral of this story: Learn to use the 10 Tests of Spiritual Discernment in Chapter 8, and learn to ask questions properly by reading *Divine Revelation*. Then you can use dowsing and other intuitive kinesiology methods to help you communicate with God.

CHANNELING ENTITIES

Over the course of one year, I got several readings from a trance channeler named Marvin. He entered a sleep-like stupor and lost consciousness while "the guides" took over his body. His head drooped and his voice became creepy and weird. After his reading, Marvin had no recollection of what had occurred.

Marvin complained that he could do few readings each day, because he became disconnected from his body, uncomfortable, disoriented, and out of control. During that year, he appeared to age quickly. His hair turned white.

After a while, I began to spontaneously receive messages from what I presumed were the same "guides," though I never went unconscious. It was not long before I started giving readings. The readings seemed positive, and I felt uplifted as I received the messages. Also, the readings appeared helpful to my clients.

However, after each reading, I felt let down and depressed, hollow and empty inside. This result is a sure sign that I was not in contact with the spiritual world, but with the astral world.

Moral of this story: Use the 10 Tests of Spiritual Discernment and avoid channeling entities. Practice safe spirituality.

PSYCHIC MANIPULATION

A woman from Seattle named Ellen was despondent about losing her husband of 30 years in a car accident four years earlier, and about her boyfriend recently dumping her. She was taking Prozac and also sought comfort with a so-called psychic named Susie Evans, who gave Ellen a crystal to wear around her neck and a small picture of a saint wrapped in cellophane. Susie predicted that the ex-boyfriend would phone her that night. He did not.

A few months later, Susie promised Ellen that she could still be reunited with her ex-boyfriend. But first, Susie needed to build a crystal and gold effigy of Ellen with her boyfriend—for the bargain price of only $14,000. Later, Susie predicted that the woman's daughter would have a fatal car crash, but, for another $25,000, Susie would prevent it. Finally, Susie convinced Ellen that, for only $100,000, she could protect her entire family forever.

Ellen was just one of Susie's victims. None of Ellen's predictions came true. Her clients just found their bank accounts plundered.[2]

In another case, Margaret Faulkner, in her late 50s, a masseuse who owned the Sunny Health Food Store in New York City, used a Ouija board that purportedly served "the good angel." Clara Hoover, a 71-year-old million-aire, heiress to a tanning industry fortune, was coerced by the Ouija to give jewelry, plus various amounts of cash, totaling $52,285, in sealed envelopes to Ms. Faulkner, which she claimed were never opened but transferred to a gypsy named Yuma in an unidentified church for transmission to "the good angel." Ms. Faulkner was found guilty of fraud.[3]

Moral of these stories: Beware of anyone who makes doom-and-gloom predictions or outrageous claims. Use the healing prayers in Chapter 7 to close off your aura and cut karmic ties with such psychics.

Entity Possession

Sharon Beekmann, author of *Enticed by the Light*, knows the dangers of channeling countless unknown astral entities. Her spirit guides, King Egglog, Seth, and Starlight, turned against her in a hellish fashion when she tried to rid herself of their influence. They continued to plague her continually with coercive telepathic messages.

When she decided to stop channeling and reject Spiritualism altogether, she found that she could not. Her mind was no longer her own. Even after becoming a born-again Christian and receiving deliverance ministry, she still could not shake these spirits. Sharon even questioned whether these Christians were really in touch with Jesus, the Holy Spirit, or with decep-tive faker spirits. Finally, she was able to overcome her living nightmare through the power of prayer.

Moral of this story: Do not allow anyone or anything to take over your body or control your mind. If entities are present, use healing prayers in Chapter 7 to heal the entities, close off your aura to the entities, and cut psychic ties with the entities.

Playing With "Spirit Friends"

Sophia, a very sensitive college student in her 20s, always dressed en-tirely in black. Urged to see a psychiatrist by her mother, Sophia protested that she did not need help. Two years earlier, after frequently consulting Ouija boards, Tarot cards, and automatic writing, she started hearing three "real nice, polite, friendly" spirits that "talked a lot—all day long." Referring to them as her "friends," she often asked for advice. When Sophia went to bed, they "said good night and stopped talking" so she could sleep. Sophia described that later "they got mean and said bad things like 'nigger' and 'you're a murderess.'"

These voices became so persistent that Sophia became exhausted and confused, and could no longer carry on a conversation. She dropped out of college. When Sophia asked the spirits to leave, they berated her even more. Sophia became ill and vomited intensely for 20 days. She was sent to a mental health institution for a year.

Sophia told the psychiatrist that she could not understand why her parents had taken her Ouija board away. However, she still did automatic writing and was "having fun" with her three spirit "friends," who had returned.[4]

Moral of this story: Do not take open your aura to unknown entities. Heal them by using the healing affirmations in Chapter 7 of this book. Use the 10 tests.

DEMONIC POLTERGEIST ACTIVITY

British photojournalist Serge Kordiev and his wife agreed to join a Satanic cult. They were chauffeured in a luxurious car to a large old house. After downing a few alcoholic beverages, they stripped nude and donned small black satin aprons. In a large room with a black floor and walls covered with red carpets, six hooded figures stood before an altar. A naked man smeared with gleaming oil appeared, flanked by two black-hooded girls. The Kordievs knelt at the altar and swore perpetual homage to Satan, signing blood oaths. They received magic names, and the naked man placed his hand on their genitals.

Without delay, Serge's business boomed, and checks started rolling in.

However, the Kordievs witnessed a Black Mass where a young girl, accused of betraying the group's secrets, served as a human altar and was raped by the Master. When the Kordievs discovered their "confirmation ceremony" would involve sexual intercourse with the Master and a High Priestess, they decided to leave the group.

This withdrawal ended their good fortune.

Serge nearly went bankrupt, and his wife experienced a psychological breakdown. One night they returned to their Kent home to find an enormous toad on the doorstep. Sounds of maniacal laughter and smashing glass disturbed their sleep. The next morning, Serge found their dog cowering in the kitchen, the studio completely demolished, and drapes and furniture strewn everywhere. The studio's barred windows, securely bolted from the inside, had broken under the weight of something bursting out (not in), and the lawn and path were littered with broken glass.

Serge stated, "I still think that somehow the incident was caused by an evil power in revenge for our breaking away from the Satanist group."[5]

Moral of this story: Demonic entities are real. Making pacts with such beings can have perilous consequences. Dabbling in occult practices is a recipe for chaos. Stay away from groups that practice black arts.

Ouija Board Murder

A jealous wife, Jacqueline consulted a Ouija board to ask questions about her 72-year-old husband, Sam. The board told her that Sam was having an affair with his secretary. Jacqueline hired a private detective, who found no proof of her allegations. However, even with this lack of evidence, she still believed the Ouija board.

One night, Jacqueline hit Sam over the head with a gun while he was sleeping. As he lay unconscious, she tied him to the bed. Then she burned Sam with a hot iron until he "confessed" his affair and promised to pay her $15,000.

As soon as Jacqueline untied him, Sam murdered her.[6]

Moral of this story: Do not use Ouija boards or other psychokinetic methods unless you have a clear inner contact, inner name, inner signal, and are skilled with the 10 Tests of Spiritual Discernment.

Extraterrestrials Among Us

The "Ashtar Command" traveled throughout the United States, calling themselves the "A-team." They wore long white robes and claimed to originate from the planet Ashtar. The "mission" of this group of nine men and women was to tell everyone that people could journey from outer space. They claimed to travel here on the astral plane. After they arrived on this planet, they magically manifested human bodies and clothes, and they all spoke English! Every one of these so-called space aliens appeared firmly convinced of this fairytale. The A-Team spent the majority of time in Sedona, Arizona, where their job was to de-program people from the effects of an evil mainframe computer in West Sedona.

Another group of extraterrestrials showed up at a New Age expo from Europe with a handy-dandy, collapsible, portable star-chamber, for traveling to other planets. This "stargate" consisted of copper tubing with crystals attached to it. The inventors of this contraption claimed to be earthlings who reinvented a so-called "Atlantian technology," which they recalled from past lives. At the expo, as newagers sat inside the chamber, these reincarnated Atlantians marched around, chanting and vocalizing strange otherworldly tones. However, much to everyone's amazement, no one traveled anywhere.[7]

Moral of this story: Never be duped by ludicrous claims of the delusional.

"Those who stand for nothing, fall for anything."
—Alexander Hamilton

GURU SNAKE OIL

Dagne Crane of Danbury, Connecticut, traveled to India to see a famous guru, desperate for a cure for her paralyzed godson. She waited three weeks to see the master, as she watched a parade of blind and handicapped stream by, none of which was cured. When she finally was granted an audience, the guru "materialized" an amethyst ring and told Dagne to hold it against the boy's severed spine.

She described, "He promised unequivocally that the boy would be totally cured and walking in fifteen days. [All of the devotees present] cried and kissed his feet, as I did." Tragically, when Dagne's godson was not cured as promised, the boy took it to be a rejection by God.[8]

Moral of this story: Use discernment when choosing health practitioners. Just because a guru has millions of followers does not prove that he has greater integrity or higher consciousness.

"If fifty million people say a foolish thing, it is still a foolish thing."
—Anatole France

PSYCHIC COERCION

At age 20, famous psychic Dion Fortune worked for "the Warden," a violent-tempered tyrant who had studied the occult in India. She terrorized her staff and extorted money from followers through mind control and hypnotic suggestion.

The Warden often filed baseless charges against employees in order to dismiss them without wages. To force Dion to testify on her behalf, the Warden stared into Dion's eyes, programming her with repetitive suggestions for hours. Completely drained, Dion felt a peculiar sensation that her feet were no longer under her body. Then she collapsed on her bed fully clothed, and slept for 15 hours at a time.

After preventing a feeble, elderly woman from granting power of attorney to the Warden, Dion tried to escape. But the Warden caught her with suitcase in hand and said, "Before you go, you have got to admit that you are incompetent and have no self-confidence." She then fixed her gaze on Dion and repeated hypnotic suggestions for four hours straight.

Thankfully, Dion heard an inner voice say, "Pretend you are beaten before you really are. Then she will let up the attack and you will be able to get away." Dion followed her inner guidance. She asked the Warden for forgiveness and promised to stay with her for the rest of her life.

A mental and physical wreck, Dion collapsed in a stupor for 30 hours. She remained semi-conscious for several days until the housekeeper revived her. Dion had no recollection of what had happened. For several days she was possessed with immeasurable fear, dry mouth, sweaty palms, thumping heart, and shallow, quick breathing.

Finally, Dion's family rescued her. However, it took nearly three years for her to recover from this psychic attack and its toll on her health.[9]

Moral of this story: Never allow anyone to control you. You are the only authority in your life, and you have the power to control your own destiny.

Out-of-Body Horror Story

Out-of-body-experiences (OBEs) are not recommended for those who want to receive messages from God or to have spiritual experiences. Leaving your body unattended while you fly about in the astral plane is not a safe practice. When you check out of the human hotel, something else can check in and take over the empty room.

Sylvan J. Muldoon, author of *The Phenomena of Astral Projection* and *Projection of the Astral Body*, reported a terrifying out-of-body experience encountering a neighbor who had recently died of cancer. Samuel had been a sadistic brute, according to his wife. During an OBE four days after the funeral, Muldoon saw "the dead man glaring at me like a maniac. I knew he meant revenge. Before I could do anything he leapt on me. We fought for a few moments—he got the better of me, as he cursed and beat me with all his might." As Muldoon tried to re-enter his physical body, Samuel clung to him. Samuel then lifted Muldoon high into the air and violently dropped him back into his body.

Moral of this story: Do not tinker with out-of-body experiences. There is no reason to ever separate your astral body from your physical body. Your soul body is already present everywhere. Therefore, by mere intention, you can travel anywhere without ever leaving your body.

THE SEDUCTIVE LURE OF FAME

Raymond, a chiropractor from Los Angeles, started experiencing intense heat radiating from his hands and blisters on his hands. The quality of his chiropractic work improved, and people were getting spontaneous healings. Patients sensed invisible people standing in the room and felt an extra hand on their body besides his.

Raymond phoned a spiritual healer, Irene, to ask for advice. As he described his experiences, a titillated excitement entered his voice. He was scared, but hooked. Irene told him to ignore these experiences, which were just phenomena, and not very interesting. She warned Raymond that this was a test to see how seduceable he was. She said, "You think they are stigmata. Wow, Christ has come. Go back to being a chiropractor. Do your normal adjustment."

Irene's advice was like telling a child not to eat chocolate. He was spellbound by fame and glamour, and he soon became the trendy Hollywood healer. With long waiting-lists, he could not rest or sleep. Finally, at wit's end, he traveled to see Irene. She said that now he had some serious problems. She warned him to return to being a real doctor or else pay grave consequences.

Raymond then took a seminar with Irene in Mount Shasta. There he told her that when he heals people, an energy overtakes him. He professed that God was flowing through him. How could this be bad? Irene responded, "What is bad is that you have identified with the entity and have now become the entity. You are on an ego trip." Then Irene's husband confiscated the tape recorder that Raymond was secretly using to tape her class.

Now a world-famous healer, Raymond stole Irene's entire healing system, while giving no credit to her.[10]

Moral of this story: Do not allow anything to take over your body, even if that thing appears to be a healing energy or a psychic surgeon.

GURU-OF-THE-MONTH CLUB

Unless you first lived thousands of lifetimes, you could not get into the room with Frederick P. Lenz (alias Zen Master Rama). When you meditated with him, the room glowed and he changed shapes and levitated—so his disciples asserted. Posters offering intensive seminars "designed specifically for men and women under 30" recruited students at college campuses.

Lenz taught computer seminars at $5,000 a pop: "the fast track to enlightenment." Barbara Sherman, former cult member, said, "He tells you where to live, what soap to buy, what movies and TV shows to watch." After taking his computer class, she slept on the floor and paid Lenz virtually everything she earned.

Lenz told his disciples to write down every night, "I will meet Rama in the desert." Then they set the alarm to wake up every two hours and check their dreams. If they were not dreaming about Lenz, they had to find him.

Only women with "rare karma" were chosen to have sex with him. So, when Lenz summoned Barbara at 11 p.m., she was thrilled. "I had waited for years for the enlightened one to recognize me." Lenz told her she lived in Atlantis, studied with him in past lives, and was very evolved. He gave her two capsules of so-called "Benadryl," which gave her strange reactions for an antihistamine. After they had sex, Barbara felt ashamed when she failed to achieve orgasm, because, when Lenz gave a woman an orgasm, he could "flip her consciousness to other dimensions."

Lenz forced members to sever ties with family and friends, and they could no longer contact anyone from their past. Married couples were separated, while Lenz had sex with all female disciples, married or not. Followers who did not tow the line were threatened with cancer in this life and hell in the next. Lenz warned that if they left the group, their lives would fall apart. If disciples doubted him, it was because of demons that made people do bad things.

Mark Laxer, a cult member for more than seven years, said Lenz knocked down self-confidence and made people fearful of everything, including going to sleep. Laxer affirmed that Lenz gave his followers LSD and took it himself.

Incredibly, Lenz's novel *Surfing the Himalayas*, which related snowboarding adventures to spirituality, reached the best-seller lists in 1995. Even worse, he was on the list of *New York* magazine's "100 Smartest New Yorkers" in 1995.

On April 11, 1998, at age 48, Frederick Lenz was found dead in Conscience Bay off Long Island, about 60 feet from land. A dog collar with an attached rabies vaccination tag encircled his neck. He had ingested 150 Phenobarbital tablets and fallen into the water from the dock at the rear of his $2 million home. A female companion and several dogs were similarly drugged, but they survived.[11]

Moral of this story: Beware of con artists with a hidden agenda who masquerade as spiritual teachers.

~~~

In the next chapter, you will read inspirational stories about listening to the "still small voice" and trusting the guidance you receive.

Chapter 11

TRUSTING DIVINE GUIDANCE

"You have to leave the city of your comfort and go into the
wilderness of your intuition. What you'll discover will be wonderful.
What you'll discover is yourself."
—Alan Alda

This chapter is a compilation of stories about hearing the voice of God.
These are true stories about real people who have taken the leap of faith to
trust that "still small voice." Realizing that God is their guide, they are willing
to follow the divine guidance they receive with total trust. Their stories will
inspire you as you further your quest to communicate directly with God.

PREMONITION OF TITANIC PROPORTIONS

Eva Miriam Hart (1905–1996), born in Ilford, Essex, England, was 7
years old when her father, Benjamin Hart, decided to immigrate to Winnipeg,
Canada, to profit from that region's construction boom. But Eva's mother,
Esther Bloomfield Hart, age 45, sensed disaster and tried to convince her
husband to change his mind.[1]

The Hart family booked passage on the ship *Philadelphia*, but, due to a coal strike, they were rescheduled for the RMS *Titanic*. Upon boarding the ship at Southampton, Esther sensed something wrong with the ship. Eva described, "We went down to the cabin and that's when my mother said to my father that she had made up her mind quite firmly that she would not go to bed in that ship, she would sit up at night. She decided that she wouldn't go to bed at night, and she didn't!"

Throughout the voyage, Esther felt a catastrophe would hit the ship at night. That is why she slept during the day and kept vigil every night. Although the *Titanic* was advertised by the White Star Lines as "unsinkable,"[2] Esther declared that to call a ship unsinkable was "flying in the face of God."

On Saturday, April 13th, Esther was awakened when she felt a "gigantic force had given the ship a mighty push behind." She heard the swirling of water and then felt "push," and heard "swirl" three times. The next morning at breakfast, her husband joked about it. However, Esther felt it was a "warning from God."[3]

That same night, April 14, 1912, the *Titanic* sank, and 1,523 lives were lost—the greatest maritime disaster of all time.[4] Benjamin Hart did not survive.

The experience of Esther Hart was not unique. Many more premonitions are described in George Behe's *Titanic: Psychic Forewarnings of a Tragedy*. Similarly, dozens of uncanny predictions of the 2001 World Trade Center attack are described in John Marquardt's *Premonitions of September 11th*.

A Dream Saved Her Life

Laura Hatch, age 17, of Redmond, Washington, was last seen leaving a party on October 2, 2004. Sha Nohr's daughter, who was Laura's classmate, plus 200 other volunteers, had been searching more than a week for her. Sha said that when her daughter showed her a photograph of Laura, "it just made me start thinking about her."

Sha posted the photo on her prayer group Website, and local churches were praying for her. One night, Sha had a dream of an intersection with which she was familiar. She saw a wooded area and heard the message, "Keep going, keep going."

Sha woke up the next day with an urgent need to look for Laura. Sha and her daughter prayed as they drove to the intersection. "I just thought, 'Let her speak out to us,'" Sha told the *Seattle Times*.

Sha stopped at one area but left because "it just didn't feel right." Then something led her to stop at another place and clamber over a concrete barrier, more than 100 feet down a steep, densely vegetated embankment off Union Hill Road. At first Sha did not see the car, hidden by several downed trees. When she managed to barely discern the wrecked Toyota Camry amid the trees, she thought Laura was dead.

When Laura started talking, Sha realized that it was a miracle and a blessing. "I told her that people were looking for her and they loved her," Sha recalled, "and she said, 'I think I might be late for curfew.'"[5]

DIVINE FIRE PREVENTION

Jeanne Webster, Otto, North Carolina

My husband, who used to work 24/7/365, was home one evening and wanted to put the kids to bed. I sure let him! Fifteen minutes after he came back downstairs, I heard an inner voice say, "Check Sara NOW." It ran through me like a bullet and I was on the stairs before taking another breath.

When I got to her room, I noticed my husband had laid a sheer scarf over her dresser lamp. It was scorched and smoking badly. I grabbed it off the lamp, opened the window, and threw it out as it was starting to produce a flame. I picked up the baby and ran out of the room.

For three days I just thanked God over and over—talk about thanking. This scared me so badly that I don't believe I let Sara's feet touch the floor for a week.

DIVINE POLICE PROTECTION

Evelyn Matthews, Mount Vernon, New York

I was working as a police officer in Port Chester, New York. My squad was dispatched in the middle of the night to a burglary in progress. Upon our arrival, we split up to check the building. I went to the right and back of a dark room.

While checking the room, Spirit told me to turn quickly to the right. As I turned, it felt like a divine presence was standing with me—not inside, but outside, all around me. At that very moment, upon turning, I saw a man rise up from behind a large box with his gun in his hand. By the time he rose all the way up, I was already facing him with my gun drawn on him.

The burglar and I locked eyes. I remained calm because Spirit told me to. I told the burglar to drop his gun. He did. I said to myself, "Thank you, God!" Then I called to the other officers that I had caught the burglar.

DIVINELY DISPELLED DANGER

Joyce Harvey, Lawrenceville, Georgia

I was merging onto the highway. I needed to quickly move three lanes to the left to access a connecting freeway. Just as I began to merge, my inner voice said, very firmly, "Stay in this lane."

I responded silently, "If I stay in this lane, I'll miss the freeway."

My inner voice was persistent, "Stay in this lane."

I stayed in the lane. Within seconds, two cars burst into flames in the exact spot I would have been, had I not listened to my inner guidance.

GUIDED BY BLIND FAITH

Maryam Balbed, Web designer, Silver Spring, Maryland

After shopping in Georgetown, I was relaxing in the picturesque gardens and old trees of Dumbarton Oaks, a 19th-century mansion on 10 acres. Suddenly I noticed a menacing-looking man urinating in public about 50 yards away. From that moment, I entered some kind of zone.

I heard a crystal-clear voice say, "Slowly grab your bag and start moving." I absolutely knew each move to make, with immediate, visceral knowing. In that "zone," I moved fast, totally focused, and reached a thicket of tall bamboo. Then I came to a patch of dense, tall plants. That's when I freaked out, because I had no idea how to find the only safe way out—toward a Georgetown supermarket.

Then I noticed a bird singing a distinct song. Call me crazy, but my inner guidance said to follow the sound of that bird. I moved in its direction. Within a few minutes I saw the supermarket, and I knew I was safe. A tall staircase lead from the gardens to the supermarket, and I ran up those stairs as fast as I could.

Until that point, I had never looked back. But when I reached the top, I looked down the stairs. The man was at the bottom of the stairs looking up at me.

SPARED FROM SPARE PARTS

Rian Leichter, engineering consultant, Woodside, California

I had an uneasy feeling about signing a contract with a particular company that wanted to sell me an entire truckload of computer parts at a cut-rate price. I did not go ahead with the deal, although it promised to save me thousands of dollars. As it turned out, my inner voice was right. I later discovered that the parts were all defective.

FINDING A LOST CHILD

Terrie Brill, Redwood Shores, California

As an intuitive astrologer, I was helping mothers locate missing children on the *Jerry Springer Show*. One of the children had run away several times—the last time from a halfway house. Her mother came on stage. I held her hand and said, "Your daughter is in a place that looks like a bar, but is not. There's a neon flashing sign. She's like a prisoner, looking through a barred window. The room is dirty like a cell, but the door is open. She could leave anytime. She's back on heavy drugs, sleeping in this filthy bed, like a cot. She's okay. She'll be back in your arms in six weeks, and she'll be fine."

Sure enough, the mother later called me: "Just like you said, there were bars on the window. She was in this dirty room that looked like a cell. And she's back in my arms and back in the halfway house."

About three years later, I appeared with the mother and daughter on the *Rolanda* show. The daughter was totally clean and back in school, having a wonderful life.

MOVED BY SPIRIT

Jenifer Whisper, San Diego, California

I was in a desperate living situation, but procrastinating about moving. The dope-filled neighborhood was getting worse. I couldn't handle it anymore. People were getting murdered. A guy jumped over the fence in our yard with cops chasing him.

One Sunday morning I woke up and sat bolt upright. Spirit yelled through me, "MOVE!" And I said, "Oh, my God, you scared me."

I attended a class at Unity Church about procrastination. After the class I drove around instead of going home. Spirit kept saying, "Go look for a house. The house is waiting for you. You have the money, and everything is okay." Sure enough, I drove to Polk and Boundary streets, and saw a house for rent. It was so cute. The owners were there, cleaning up the yard, so I rented it on the spot.

Finally, I went home. John was watching a football game. I said, "I found a house, and I'm moving. If you want, you can move with me." John didn't want to move, so I moved and got out of the relationship.

GOD GAVE ME THE WRITE ANSWER

Vicki Jenkins, Columbus, Ohio

It was the end of the year of my first year of law school during the only test for the year for the only course on contracts. I was halfway through the final examination, and as I was writing the answer to a question, suddenly the "correct" answer came to me.

I had to literally start all over. I quickly grabbed additional pieces of paper and began to write the correct answer. My hand was moving very quickly across the page, as the correct answer poured out. I did not know exactly what I was writing, but I knew it was the right answer. The answer was not necessarily in my head. It was flowing out of the pen in my hand, and I just let the answer come. I wondered if I could get it all out before the exam ended. I finished writing just as the professor stated that time for the exam had ended.

When I received my grades during the summer, I got an A in the class. Upon returning to school in the fall, my contracts professor told me that the answer I gave was the one he was looking for, and that I was the only student who had provided that answer.

A Bomb Threat

Gaelia Babineau, Albuquerque, New Mexico

I came to work late, and all the employees from the three-story building were assembled in the parking lot. My boss said to me, "Go take lunch. You can have two lunch breaks, one now and one at the normal time." I asked, "What's going on?" He said, "It's a bomb threat."

I asked my inner guidance and got the message that there was no bomb. It was a sunny day and I would have welcomed time off. But I had to finish a ton of work before leaving on vacation the following week.

The police had already searched the building, but the employees were waiting for some bomb detection device to sweep the building. I wanted to go to work, so I did. Two co-workers came after me and tried to pull me out. I told them, "Go away. I'm not dumb; I know what I'm doing. There's no bomb in this building."

After the bomb scare was over, my boss, a conservative attorney, came into my office and said, "I heard you were here earlier." I answered, "Yes, I've been here since 1:00." He asked, "Who did you talk to—God?" I had been pretty straight with him up until that point, so I said, "As a matter of fact, yes."

> IMPORTANT: Gaelia had been receiving clear divine guidance for more than 20 years. Therefore, she had the clarity of discernment to know that the message was accurate. However, the author does not recommend that you, as reader, follow any apparently dangerous guidance yourself. Please study and use the 10 tests in Chapter 8.

Bless Others and Be Blessed

Edward Overton, physician, Birmingham, Alabama

While I was in jail, I was able to touch a few lives. Wade had been told to read *Celestine Prophesy* by James Redfield, but couldn't get a copy. He was then transferred to another prison, where a young man walked up to him and handed him the book! He started reading it, but was transferred again before he finished. So when I suggested he read the same book, it was a sign that something was going on!

We spent two months together, and I was afraid I would not be able to break him out of his ennui. Finally, two weeks ago, I told him I felt he was to be a spiritual leader, to his children if no one else, and I needed to teach him the Divine Revelation techniques. Wade had not been open to it before. But when he recognized the synchronicity of being told to read the same book in three different jails, he opened his mind and spirit.

We had a nice meditation, and he made contact. I received guidance that now that he had his breakthrough, he would not be required to do any prison time. He didn't believe me, but two days later, his judge vacated all 14 years, including probation, and reduced his sentence to a fine. He was given work release to allow him to come up with the money to pay his fine. Then he will be out.

It was only after Wade had his breakthrough that all of my legal problems fell to the wayside. The next day, my case was taken away from the judge who was refusing to do anything, and the new judge read the motion to dismiss my charges that had been sitting there for over two months. Fully a month ahead of the hearing date that she set, she released me and dismissed all charges against me.

Prophetic Dream About My Baby

Deja Laufer, Saratoga, California

I was due to have a baby about the beginning of September. One of my closest girlfriends, who is into this teaching, called me one day and told me she had a dream that my baby would be born on the same day as her daughter, and that I would have a girl. I told her, "That's impossible. That would make me two and a half weeks late. That's a long time past my due date." She said, "Well, that's what I dreamed."

Sure enough, my daughter was born on the same day as her daughter.

Warnings Despite Appearances

Sydney Chase, Half Moon Bay, California

I was offered a position at a vocational college in San Jose where I had worked before, and where many of my friends continued to work. I left the job interview really high and excited. As I drove over the mountain and arrived home, I was still high, but also felt a foreboding. I realized, "Something is wrong here." So the next morning I called and said, "Thank you, but I thought about this overnight, and I'm going to pass on the opportunity." I didn't know if I did the right thing. I just followed that inner voice.

A year later, I went to dinner with my friends working at the college. They groaned about the hell of the situation. They were overworked and miserable, never good enough and never did enough. They had all gained 30 to 40 pounds. Their boss was abusive—emotionally and verbally. But he hooked them by paying a salary that nobody else in the industry would pay. Then he just abused the hell out of them.

It was a good salary and benefits, and a beautiful working environment. The people all seemed warm and couldn't have been more charming and exciting on the surface. There was nothing that said I should turn down this job. It seemed the answer to all my problems. The feelings were high, but I acted on that inner voice. Sometimes that's hard. It requires a lot of discipline.

WAKE UP AND SMELL THE ROSES

Annette Gore, Bella Vista, Arkansas

I am a real estate agent in Bentonville, Arkansas. My inner guidance told me to move my office from Exit Pinnacle realty back to Remax. All the people at Exit realty were attached to me, as I was to them. My broker at Exit didn't want me to leave and offered me outrageous perks that no one in her right mind would turn down.

The other agents in the office were crying because I was leaving, and I was crying, too. I left the Exit Pinnacle office very upset. I packed the last vestiges of my office, a few computers, into my car in the parking lot, and was ready to drive to the Remax office. I got into my car, closed my eyes, leaned my head on the steering wheel, and said, "Oh my God, am I insane? I must be crazy to turn down what the broker offered. Have I made the right decision?"

At that moment, a profound calm overtook me. A strong fragrance of roses, my signal for Mother Mary, wafted through my car. I wondered whether I possibly smelled the poinsettia plant in the cargo section at the back of my car. But I soon realized these roses were not of this world.

As I relaxed into the wave of divine energy that swept over me, Mother Mary said, "I love you so much. You are doing exactly as instructed. You are on the right path." This experience gave me total confidence that I had made the right decision.

Now that I am back at Remax, my business is back on track.

MY DIVINE PIANO TEACHER

A.H. Onaran, concert pianist, New York, New York

My 83-year-old piano teacher had to return home to Argentina. After my last lesson with her, I walked home depressed, unfocussed, and moody. I asked, "Lord, what will I do now? Show me the way. I need somebody I can trust to have communication with."

I arrived home at the time I usually practice meditation, but instead my inner voice said, "Turn on the television." I switched around with the remote. On a cable channel a woman was talking about piano and music. After the third time through the channels, I finally thought, "Wait a minute. She's talking about very interesting things." So I started watching.

Within five minutes I knew she would be my next teacher. I didn't know her qualifications or anything. But my inner voice said, "This is it. This is what you've been wanting." So I wrote her name down and phoned her.

I feel that all this time was a preparation for this teacher. The progress I've made is incredible. There's a real communication between us, and she's very spiritual. I'm glad I listened to my inner voice.

MY DIVINE GPS

Dan Ecklund, Foley, Alabama

At my pizza delivery job, I was looking for addresses to deliver my pizzas. Unfamiliar with the two streets I had drawn, I could either return to base to consult a map, or trust inner guidance to find the proper location. I decided to test my use of Divine Revelation, and continued driving in the direction where I felt the first one might be.

I found the street, but couldn't find the house. I asked people for directions to the address, but no one knew where it was. Then I asked God to help me. I got an impression to turn at a nearby intersection. I did so, and immediately saw the continuation of the street. The house was easily found.

Then I took off in the direction where I felt the second house was, off one of two main north-south streets. I received an impression after praying, and continued to the one indicated. Then I drove along until I felt where to turn. There were no street signs, but I followed my inner guidance.

Not seeing any house numbers in this new development, I asked passersby for help. They told me I was on the correct street, and the house was behind me. Indeed, I saw an adolescent boy standing in one driveway, waving me down.

I have determined that this tool, Divine Revelation, is sufficient to get me to any destination or conclusion that I need to reach. While setting out blindly on a journey might be considered foolish, it is a useful tool for stretching my revelatory muscles, and increasing my faith in God's ability to guide me.

"I Am There"

James Dillet Freeman, Poet Laureate, Unity Church

My first wife, Catherine, was sick, so I took her to a doctor. Then I went to pray for her in the Silent Unity Prayer Room in Kansas City. As I turned toward the prayer room in fear and agony, suddenly I heard an audible voice— so audible that I looked around to see who was there.

The voice said: "Do you need me? I am there." As I sat down, the voice began to speak again. I always have a pad and pencil in my pocket, so I wrote down the words as they came.

Several weeks later I showed the poem to Martha Smock, editor of *Daily Word*. She said, "Let's print it, Jim." I am glad we did. Nothing I have written has helped more people. It even helped an astronaut, Col. James Irwin. He carried it with him on his *Apollo 15* journey to the moon. When he returned to earth, he visited me at Unity Village.

This is the only time I heard an audible voice. All I had to do was write, word for word, what the voice said. However, every time I write, I pray for the words I need, and I open my heart and mind to God's inspiration and guidance. Most of the time, thank God, the words come quickly and easily. I always keep writing until the words come that say what God wants me to say.

God is speaking. Are you listening?[6]

In the next chapter, you will read stories and testimonials that will help you live every precious moment in the heart of God.

Chapter 12
LIVING *in the* HEART *of* GOD

"But if from thence thou shalt seek the Lord thy God, thou shalt find him,
if thou seek him with all thy heart and with all thy soul."
—Deuteronomy 4:29

The secret of how to attain a clear spiritual connection is epitomized by the following letter from Lorraine Collins of Sacramento, California, a single mother who had read *Divine Revelation*: "After my divorce I was desperate and alone. Broken and bewildered, I thought everyone had abandoned me. In my darkest hour, something astonishing happened. I suddenly remembered what you wrote. If I was ever in trouble, I could call on my higher self for help. I felt silly doing it, but I sat down in a chair and said, through my tears, 'If you exist, dear Spirit, then please come now and help me.' Within a few moments a kind of peace and comfort swept through me. Where before I felt so sad, now an inner joy or light came into my mind. I'll never forget the feeling."

The remainder of this chapter is filled with precious spiritual experiences of people who have connected with God intimately by using the methods in this book.

My New Life in God's Presence

Ken Krueger, carpenter, Watertown, Wisconsin

Your book has opened my eyes and heart to God. I meditate every morning. I feel the power of God and got the signals for the master teachers in me. Now I feel the presence of Jesus, a strong relationship with Mother Mary—my primary teacher—Holy Spirit, and a master you call Babaji. He is with me every day, and every day I ask him why he is there and the answer I always get is "to let you know that God is a lot bigger than you can believe and he is the God of everyone."

The meditation and presence of God is overwhelming, and I listen closely for any guiding messages. Thank you for your help in my finding the true God within me, the loving God, not the vengeful God that was so much a part of my youth.

Christ Consciousness

Mussa, San Jose, California

Since I started studying this teaching, Spirit has been teaching me to listen to my heart and to feel as well as reason with my mind. Recently I have started to experience living in the Christ Consciousness.

My first experience happened one day after leaving work. As I walked through a sidewalk fair, I felt a feeling of unconditional love for everyone I met. I saw the world through the eyes of Christ and loved everyone and everything. Everything was so beautiful and I felt so childlike and trusting, that I was overcome. This state was so wonderful that it seemed a bit overwhelming. Since my first experience with the Christ consciousness, I have had other similar amazing experiences.

Divine Power and Energy

Thaddeus Sun Sheng Cai, student, Singapore

I can feel God's love growing stronger within my heart each day. I am full of joy and I understand very well the importance of "living in the now." I can feel the power of God's glory shining through me. That's because, from the first breakthrough, I have developed myself into a better person with constant nurture and care, and am currently still fighting like a soldier to keep my mind clear and rested, and I have been using the healing prayers almost every day.

The last message I received very clearly from divine spirit while I was walking to school was, "Ye shall see my glory and power with time." I spoke the message aloud. At the same time I felt a surge of energy up my spine and onto the back of my head. I could feel tingling sensations in my head, a light and buoyant feeling. I felt powerful, strong, inspired, assured, peaceful, and happy. The inner knowingness made me feel compelled to live God's truth each day and prepare myself for the future and trust in God.

ONE WITH THE LIGHT

Paul Campbell, civil engineer, Singapore

During my Divine Revelation breakthrough, when I walked through the gate into Spirit, there was a host of angels waiting for me. The background was black and the angels were subtle shapes. I was traveling through this universe escorted by the angels. On the horizon, there was a sun, and as I journeyed past the sun, the light arose as if it were sunrise, until I was surrounded by and part of the light. The light was subtle and loving. I was one with the light.

FILLED WITH LIGHT

Albert Marsh, retired architect, Los Angeles, California

As I listened to a talk by a dynamic, charismatic woman minister from Salt Lake City, I became aware that the room was getting brighter and brighter, as if someone had turned on more lights. The light in the room transformed until the room disappeared into a beautiful golden mist. I was lifted into ecstasy and my consciousness expanded. It was so wonderful that there was not a thought of fear or resistance. My mind opened wide.

Then all my questions were answered. I understood how the universe works in all its details—a perfect, eternal self-sustaining system. I understood why we are here. I understood the function of all the masters, angels, and higher selves, and how they come to lift us into union with God. But this was beyond understanding. It was an actual experience of all that and much more. I was filled with love and power. Totally unaware of myself and my surroundings, I was crying with the intensity of love that I was feeling. I was so blessed to have it happen to me.

I went back to my life, but I can say for sure that I no longer looked at it in the same way. I had undeniable evidence of the presence of Spirit in my life. From then on, my belief was grounded in my experience.

My Deepest Meditation

Victor Cox, Dallas, Texas

I went into the deepest meditation I have ever experienced in my life. I cannot fully express with words the feelings I had. Frankly, I'm not sure exactly how I got there. I felt a wonderfully blissful, expanding feeling inside of me, like something was within me. I asked, "Who are you?"

"I am the divine light inside you. I am your divine teacher," was the response. I saw nothing, but I sensed the presence of many people. I said, "The people, Lord—who are all the people?"

"They are your friends. They are here to welcome you." I was then welcomed by each one of them, but I was not given any names.

I asked several more questions and received answers to these, too. I did not want to leave, but I came out of meditation, and felt myself trembling. As I went back to bed, I looked at the clock, and at least 45 minutes had passed. I could not believe I had been in that state for that long. I feel that God has sent me to you. Thank you, Susan.

Redefining Spirituality

Nyree Sessions, Sydney, Australia

I spent more than a decade in a "born again" Christian church. I was the role-model Christian, tireless servant, and leader. When I left seven years ago, I was treated like a modern-day leper, "backslider," and "sinner." I had been taught that by not going to church, I couldn't have a relationship with God, and, even worse, I was now going to hell for my transgressions.

Dr. Shumsky has helped me redefine my understanding of God. She has freed my mind and enabled my spirit to commune with God once again. I know that I know that I know that I am on the path again to joy and peace.

I thank her for showing me that a real God also exists outside the church— one that is loving and won't send me to hell. I am experiencing a loving God again, one who I once knew, who wants to communicate with me just where I am. I am still healing and many old belief patterns are still being lovingly broken down. But I feel that I am recapturing a communion with God without fear, doubt, or guilt.

Rediscovering God

Maryam Balbed, Silver Spring, Maryland

When I was 15, a very confused and cruel man (a cult leader) had me convinced that I had left God and lost God forever. I developed a real connection with God in the cult, and, over the years after I left, I was in and out of churches trying to find that connection again, but I never felt it the same.

When I was exposed to metaphysical teachings, I met a lot of wonderful people—and a lot of people with ego issues. And almost all that I met would talk about "spirit" or "the universe," but never God. It seemed to be not okay to talk about God too much. But it was God that I needed.

From what I'm reading in Susan Shumsky's books, for the first time since I left the cult, I feel as if God has been given back to me. I was 15 when I left the cult and I'm 46 now. That's a long time to wait.

Discovering My Inner Christ

Tim Smith, minister, Boynton Beach, Florida

I am a minister from a traditional Christian background, with several degrees from the most conservative Southern Baptist Seminary in the United States. I recently made a commitment to practice and work on seeking my inner truth. When I found Dr. Shumsky's book *Divine Revelation*, I began to practice the teaching of the book. However, I had been so hung up on my experience with the whole "Christian Church" that I had no concept of an inner Christ. Imagine Christ living in my heart—not a difficult, new concept—yet very new to me indeed. Now that I think about it, it is bizarre to not have an inner Christ. It all made such perfect sense when I made a decision to seek the Christ self as the book instructed.

When I went there to seek that and to ask for it, I received it. The inner Christ self revealed itself to me. It spoke to me in a clear voice a message of love and acceptance, telling me that it had been there all along and loved me regardless of my circumstances. I have gotten what I have asked for any time that I ask.

I have avoided the Bible for many years because I felt betrayed by it. Now the scriptures that I've studied thus far are all coming to life through this revelation of the inner Christ self and my God self. I am growing and changing on a daily basis. I can truly say that during each meditation I go deeper and deeper into my inner self than ever in my life.

My Revelation of God

Stuart Van Niekerk, English teacher, Scotland

After years of meditation; accepting Buddhist vows to not drink, smoke, and so on; and then going to the opposite extreme for four months in Mexico of smoking three joints a day, and getting nowhere, I went into a bathroom at the Guadalajara airport, bowed my head, and said, "God, I don't know if there is a God, but if there is, please show me, and I will change my life."

A perfect peace descended on me and into my heart. I walked out of that bathroom, born again in that moment. I just knew there was a God and that He was walking with me every step of the way.

I walked up to the basin and a young Mexican boy with a small, hand-made, wooden cross around his neck, and a big smile. He asked me, "Agua, señor?" I answered, "Sí, por favor." He turned on the water faucet into my life, face, and whole being. Picture crystal-clear waters flowing through me. All fear left me at that moment.[1]

Be Still

Andrew Sanderson, real estate appraiser, New Zealand

My divine guidance tells me to "be still" as the solution to everything. I know this is good advice and I was really happy with it because I was a real renunciate, craving silence and solitude. I found the Vedanta teachings of Ramana Maharshi and Shankara so soothing, clear, and easy to understand. Even now they give me a thrill. But now I want to engage in this *mithya* (world of illusion). Yet my intuition says that focusing on the absolute is better, because it is the only thing that will satisfy me. Part of me wants to grow, play, explore, and heal my body and emotions. But my intuition always says that I should first just be still. I can't argue with good advice.

Heaven on Earth

Elizabeth Wilson, aesthetician, Westminster, California

I just can't express the amount of joy, love, respect, hope, trust, compassion, protection, and approval I'm feeling from our Heavenly Creator right now. Just the other day I was driving to my volunteer job and was looking at the trees and the birds, the people on the side of the street holding their shopping bags and children waiting for the bus, smiling from the love of all and thought, "My God, I'm living heaven on earth right here, right now!" To have been delivered from the gates of hell (living in fear) to enjoying absolutely every moment that I breathe is, by far, my concept of heaven. And to have this now in my life—I'm speechless!

IN THE FLOW

P.J. Worley, real estate investor, Woodside, California

In listening and following my guidance, I think it's the seemingly little things that are particularly precious, because they keep me aware of the flow, put a smile in my heart, and lift my Soul. Like everything else in life, you get what you ask for, which is a fundamental reason goal-setting is valued and promoted in many professional environments. By paying attention and using your inner sensing, promptings, and inspirations, it becomes a habit, a way of being, and you use it more often. For example, you are thinking, "I want a parking place, and in front would be nice." You get to use your inner sensing a whole lot more when you ask.

Remembering to ask is what's important and helpful. I've noticed that you always get the parking space, true, but it's not always where you think it should be. And it's fun to discover there is a reason, apparent or not, but mostly apparent. You may think, "This is strange," but go with the flow and get out of the car, and there's someone you're supposed to talk with or meet at the divine right time. Or maybe the spot is in front of a place where you're reminded to do something or buy something. So there's an element of asking, an element of acceptance, and an element of confidence in the knowledge you're where you're supposed to be, and the people in your life are there on purpose. One of my favorite affirmations is "I AM in the perfect right place at the perfect right time, expressing and experiencing Divine process and manifesting Divinely perfect results."

THE GOD CONNECTION

Michael Terranova, spiritual teacher, Vancouver, Washington

Once people have the connection, it's not a big deal. It's like breathing. It's like going to the store and finding the cake you've been looking for forever. It adds so much to peace of mind. I still get upset, and I still do all the things that everybody does, but I have that spiritual anchor that just brings me back—always brings me back. I'm just so happy to have gone through the teaching and know what I know. When people get their connection, it is just great.

God has no body now on earth, but yours,
No hands but yours, no feet but yours.
Yours are the eyes through which
God's compassion looks out on the world.
Yours are the feet with which
God is to go about doing good.
Yours are the hands with which
God is to bless the people.
—St. Theresa of Avila

Epilogue

At the center of your being is a treasure trove beyond anything you could imagine. It is the "pearl of great price"—the treasure beyond all seeking, the place of perfect peace, and the home that you have longed for. It is God's holy presence within. There is no greater love than this, no greater comfort, no greater joy.

Dive into this perfect place of peace, the precious pool at the center of your being, where God is, and bathe in the waters of life. Allow the cool waters of God's precious love to wash over you and cleanse you. Remove all dross, all that is not of truth. Bathe in the comfort of God's love. Be blessed in God's holy presence.

There is nowhere to go, nothing to seek. This place of perfect content is the only fulfillment. Now you realize that there is nothing to compare with God's precious gift, the gift of unconditional love. God is the goal of all seeking. God is the oneness, the perfection, the wholeness.

This teaching is a precious gift to every one of you who has read this book. This is the most valued jewel that you have sought for many lifetimes. Take this gift and use it to achieve the greatest reward of all: God realization. You have the power to experience God. You have the desire to become all that you can be. With the tools in this book, you now have the means. Trust in God to guide you, and be at peace.

"I found I had less and less to say,
until finally, I became silent,
and began to listen.
I discovered in the silence
the voice of God."
—Soren Kierkegaard

Notes

Chapter 1: God Can Talk to You
1. Matthew 7:7.

Chapter 3: The Answer to Everything
1. Jeremiah 23: 23–24.
2. Acts 17:28.
3. II Chronicles 15:2.
4. Luke 17:21.
5. Joshua 1:5.
6. Exodus 33:11.
7. *Bhagavad Gita* 6:18–20.
8. Aitareya Upanishad 3.3.
9. Brihadaranyaka Upanishad 1.4.10.
10. Chandogya Upanishad 6.8.7.
11. Chandogya Upanishad 3.14.1.
12. Mandukya Upanishad 1.2.

Chapter 4: The Four Signposts of Spirit
1. John 1:1.
2. Psalm 33:6.
3. *The Avadhuta Gita*, 4:15. Keshavadas, Sadguru Sant. *Sadguru Dattatreya*.
4. Maitrayana Brahmaya Upanishad, 6:23.
5. espiristu@hotmail.com.
6. Matthew 7:7.

Chapter 5: The Do-Nothing Way to Meditate
1. Genesis 3:14.
2. Matthew 7:7.
3. espiristu@hotmail.com.

Chapter 6: All That Glitters Is Not God
1. Kardec, *The Spirits Book*, 40–47.

Chapter 7: Clearing the Pathway to God
1. Brihadaranyaka Upanishad, 4.4.5.
2. Proverbs 23:7.

3. Matthew 8:13.
4. Matthew 7:7.

Chapter 8: 10 Tests of Spiritual Discernment
1. Roberts, "A Linguistic," 64–65.

Chapter 9: Testing the Message
1. Matthew 5:45.
2. Cult Education and Recovery.
3. Ebon, *The Satan Trap*, 101–102.

Chapter 10: Misadventures in Psychic Delusion
1. Personal testimonial recorded by author, February 3, 2008.
2. Fitten, "$14,000," B1–B2.
3. "A $59,285," 43.
4. Ebon, *The Satan Trap*.
5. Ebon, *The Satan Trap*, 64–65.
6. Ebon, *The Satan Trap*, 172.
7. Personal testimonial recorded by author, May 3, 2004.
8. Ebon, *The Satan Trap*, 63-64.
9. Fortune, *Psychic Self-Defense*, 12–18.
10. Personal testimonial recorded by author, October 25, 2006.
11. Ex-Cult Resource Center Website.

Chapter 11: Trusting Divine Guidance
1. Deem, "ESP and the Titanic."
2. Behe, "How the Titanic Became Unsinkable."
3. "Titanic Passengers."
4. BBC, "Titanic Lives."
5. *Anderson Cooper 360 Degrees*, CNN Transcripts.
6. Freeman, *Love Is Strong As Death*. Reprinted with permission from Unity, *www.unityonline.org*.

Chapter 12: Living in the Heart of God
1. espiristu@hotmail.com.

Bibliography

Books

Beekmann, Sharon. *Enticed by the Light: The Terrifying Story of One Woman's Encounter With the New Age*. Grand Rapids, Mich.: Zondervan, 1997.

Behe, George. *Titanic: Psychic Forewarnings of a Tragedy*. Locust Valley, N.Y.: Aqua Quest Publications, 1989.

Besant, Annie. *The Bhagavad Gita*. Adyar, Madras, India: Theosophical Publishing House, 1973.

Ebon, Martin, ed. *The Satan Trap: Dangers of the Occult*. Garden City, N.Y.: Doubleday and Co., Inc., 1976.

Fiore, Edith. *The Unquiet Dead: A Psychologist Treats Spirit Possession*. New York: Ballantine Books, 1995.

Fortune, Dion. *Psychic Self-Defense*. New York: Weiser Books, 2001.

Freeman, James Dillet. *Love Is Strong As Death: Moving Through Grief*. Unity Books, 1999.

Holy Bible, The. Iowa Falls, Iowa: World Bible Publishers, no date.

Kardec, Alan. *The Spirits Book*. London: Psychic Press Ltd, 1898, 1975.

Karyalaya, Gobind Bhawan. *The Bhagavadgita*. Gorakhpur, U.P. India: Gita Press, 1984.

Keshavadas, Sadguru Sant. *Sadguru Dattatreya*. Oakland, Calif.: Vishwa Dharma Publications, 1988.

Lungin, Tatiana. *Wolf Messing: The True Story of Russia's Greatest Psychic*. St. Paul, Minn.: Paragon House Publishers, 1989.

Mahesh Yogi, Maharishi. *Bhagavad Gita, a New Translation and Commentary with Sanskrit Text*. Los Angeles, Calif.: International SRM Publications, 1967.

Makeever, Ann Meyer. *Self Mastery in the Christ Consciousness*. Lemon Grove, Calif.: Dawning Publications, 1989.

Marquardt, John. *Premonitions of September 11th*. Boca Raton, Fla.: Universal Publishers, 2002.

Meyer, Ann P., and Peter V. Meyer. *Being A Christ!* Lemon Grove, Calif.: Dawning Publications, 1988.

Moody, Raymond. *Life After Life*. New York: Bantam Books, 1980.

Muldoon, Sylvan, and Hereward Carrington. *The Phenomena of Astral Projection*. Rider & Co., 1987.

Shumsky, Susan G. *Divine Revelation*. New York: Fireside, 1996.

————. *Exploring Auras*. Franklin Lakes, N.J.: New Page Books, 2005.

————. *Exploring Chakras*. Franklin Lakes, N.J.: New Page Books, 2003.

————. *Exploring Meditation*. Franklin Lakes, N.J.: New Page Books, 2001.

————. *Miracle Prayer*. Berkeley, Calif.: Celestial Arts, 2006.

Yogananda, Paramahansa. *Autobiography of a Yogi*. Los Angeles, Calif.: Self-Realization Fellowship, 2006.

Periodicals

"A $59,285 Request by a Ouija Board Ruled Fraud Here," *New York Times*, March 3, 1970: 43.

Fitten, Ronald K. "$14,000 to retrieve boyfriend? Psychic accused of bilking women out of $92,000." *The Seattle Times*, August 27, 1996: B1–B2.

Roberts, Marjory. "A Linguistic 'Nay' to Channeling." *Psychology Today* (October 1989): 64–65.

Internet Sites

Anderson Cooper 360 Degrees. CNN Transcripts. *transcripts.cnn.com/TRANSCRIPTS/0410/12/acd.01.html*.

BBC. "Titanic Lives." *www.bbc.co.uk/kent/history/features/titanic.shtml*.

Behe, George. "How the Titanic Became Unsinkable." George Behe's Titanic Tidbits. *ourworld.compuserve.com/homepages/Carpathia/page2.htm*.

Cult Education and Recovery. *www.culteducation.com/hgate.html*.

Deem, James M. "ESP and the Titanic." *www.jamesmdeem.com/titanic1.htm*.

Ex-Cult Resource Center. *www.ex-cult.org/Groups/Rama/index.html*.

Freedom of Mind Center. *www.freedomofmind.com/resourcecenter/groups/r/rama/*.

Freeman, James Dillet. "Life Is a Wonder." *jamesdilletfreeman.wwwhubs.com/freeman5.htm*.

Hinduism Today. *www.hinduismtoday.com/archives/1997/7/1997-7-12.shtml*.

Quotations Page, The. *www.quotationspage.com*.

Sacred Text Archive. The Upanishads, Part I, translated by Max Muller. *www.sacred-texts.com/hin/sbe01/index.htm*.

Sacred Text Archive. The Upanishads, Part II, translated by Max Muller. *www.sacred-texts.com/hin/sbe15/sbe15076.htm*.

Susan Shumsky. Divine Revelation. *www.divinerevelation.org*.

Titanic Passengers. *www.titanic-passengers.com/evahart.htm*.

Index

About the Author

Dr. Susan Shumsky, foremost spirituality expert, pioneer in the personal development field, highly acclaimed and greatly respected professional speaker, Doctor of Divinity, and COVR award-winning, best-selling author of *Divine Revelation*, *Miracle Prayer*, *Exploring Meditation*, *Exploring Chakras*, and *Exploring Auras*, has practiced self-development disciplines since 1967.

Her personal mentor was enlightened spiritual master from India, Maharishi Mahesh Yogi, founder of Transcendental Meditation, guru of the Beatles and Deepak Chopra. Dr. Shumsky lived in Maharishi's ashrams in secluded areas, including the Himalayas of India and the Swiss Alps, for 20 years, and was on his personal staff for seven of those years. Then she studied New Thought and metaphysics for another 20 years.

Since 1970, Dr. Shumsky has taught yoga, meditation, prayer, and intuition to thousands of students in the United States, Canada, Europe, and the Far East. She is the founder of Divine Revelation®, a complete technology for contacting the divine presence and listening to the voice of God.

Dr. Susan Shumsky now travels full time, conducting seminars, retreats, media appearances, and tours to sacred sites worldwide. Dr. Shumsky also offers spiritual coaching, prayer therapy sessions, and breakthrough sessions.

On our Website, *www.divinerevelation.org*, you can:

- Join our mailing list.
- See Dr. Shumsky's itinerary.
- Invite Dr. Shumsky to speak to your group.
- Find Divine Revelation teachers in your area.
- See the Divine Revelation curriculum.
- Register for Divine Revelation retreats and Teacher Training Courses.
- Order books, audio and video products, or home study courses.
- Register for telephone sessions and teleconferences with Dr. Shumsky.
- Register for spiritual tours to sacred destinations worldwide.

When you join our mailing list at *www.divinerevelation.org*, you will receive a free, downloadable, guided mini-meditation, plus access to our free weekly teleconference prayer circle, our free educational teleseminars, and our free online group listserve forum.

As a gift for reading this book, please use the following special discount code when you register for one of our retreats or tours at *www.divinetravels.com*: GODSVOICE108.

We want to hear from you. Please write to us your personal experiences of hearing the voice of God: Teaching of Intuitional Metaphysics, P.O. Box 7185, New York, NY 10116, 212-946-5132, or e-mail divinerev@aol.com.